Amazing Miracles of Padre Pio

and the stories behind them

Frank M. Rega

Copyright © 2019 Frank M. Rega

All rights reserved.

ISBN: 9781070321103

The photo on the back cover of the author in his study was taken by Patricia Rega.

DEDICATION

This book is especially dedicated to those who do not yet believe in miracles.

The Picture

The picture on the following page is a painting by Italian artist Antonio Ciccone, showing Padre Pio healing a possessed woman. The story behind the picture and the artist's friendship with Padre Pio are presented in Chapter XVIII.

The Healing. 1964. Oil tempera. Canvas on board.

TABLE OF CONTENTS

	Introduction	
I	Padre Pio's First Public Miracle	1
II	A Saint on My Back	7
III	Photos of Padre Pio Came up Blank	17
IV	The Labyrinth	23
V	Padre Pio's Bilocations to Irene Gaeta	31
VI	Under the Protection of Padre Pio	39
VII	The Cure that Should Not Be	45
VIII	His Twelve Apostles	53
IX	He Shuffled There	61
X	Anatomy of a Conversion	69
XI	He Wanted to Kick Padre Pio	77
XII	Padre Pio's Masterpiece	87
XIII	She Was Cured Twice by Padre Pio	95
XIV	Padre Pio and the Angels	101
XV	Padre Pio and the Anglican Minister	109
XVI	The Mangiapreti	117
XVII	The Cure of a Desperate Illness	121
XVIII	The Artist and Padre Pio	127
XIX	He Bilocates to the Pope	135
XX	Journey into Creation	141
XXI	He Felt the Pains of Purgatory	151
XXII	He Corrects a Mischievous Boy	159
XXIII	Padre Pio Crowned with Thorns	165
XXIV	Padre Pio Hitches a Ride	169
XXV	The Doubting Thomas	173
XXVI	Padre Pio Saved His Life	179

XXVII	At the Threshold of Paradise	183
XXVIII	The Great Easter Miracle	191
XXIX	The Power of His Relic	197
XXX	He saw Jesus in Padre Pio	207
	Novena Prayer of Padre Pio	213
	Bibliography	215
	About the Author	219

INTRODUCTION

One of the greatest figures of the twentieth century was Padre Pio, a Catholic priest and wonder-worker who bore the wounds of Christ, the stigmata. In 2002 the Church raised him to the altars of sainthood, proclaiming him St. Pio of Pietrelcina.

He was born as Francesco Forgione on May 25, 1887 in a small, impoverished farming community in central Italy called Pietrelcina. A Capuchin Franciscan friar used to come to the town asking for alms, and he sported a flourishing beard, so young Francesco decided he wanted to be a friar with a beard. His parents were very pious and supported their son's interest in the religious life. In fact, his father emigrated to America twice in order to earn money so that Francesco could study for the priesthood. He entered the Franciscan Order and was given the name of Pio, and was ordained a Capuchin priest in 1910.

Around that same time, he began to experience the wounds of Christ in his hands, but he prayed that they would be invisible in order not to attract attention to himself. During his formative years, he wrote many letters to priests and his spiritual children regarding the interior life, and the four-volume collection of them is already a spiritual classic. In 1918 he received two supernatural gifts while assigned to the friary in San Giovanni Rotondo. The first was the "transverberation," consisting of a bleeding wound over his heart. A month later, he received open wounds on his hands and feet, thus becoming the first Catholic priest gifted with the stigmata.

As word of his spirituality, miracles and the stigmata spread, crowds besieged the small monastery. He became renowned as a confessor and spiritual guide. At the same time, opposition to him grew, with many saying that he was a false mystic who faked his stigmata. Eventually the Vatican placed many restrictions on his ministry, including the prohibition of writing any more letters, and even kept him from saying Mass in public for two years. But he was eventually exonerated from the false accusations and was left in relative peace for many years, until Pope John XXIII renewed the persecutions when Padre Pio was an old man.

During World War II, many US servicemen were stationed in southern Italy, and heard about a miracle-working friar in the area. They began to visit the monastery, and when they returned home after the war, many of them gave talks about Padre Pio and thus his fame in America began. In the 1950's Padre Pio saw his plans and work towards a great, new hospital in San Giovanni Rotondo come to fruition. Known as the Home for the Relief of Suffering, it has become one of the most important and best equipped hospitals in Europe. Quite an accomplishment for a sequestered monk!

I personally believe that all of the stories and events in this book are true, otherwise I would not have included them. His supernatural gifts are many and profound, and as you will see, some of them cannot fit into any known categories.

One final note: Padre Pio never attributed the working of miracles to himself, but referred all the glory, praise and thanksgiving to God, to prayer, and to the intercession of the Blessed Virgin Mary.

I. PADRE PIO'S FIRST PUBLIC MIRACLE

One of the very first newspaper articles about Padre Pio was written by Renato Trevisani for the "Mattino" of Naples, and appeared in the editions of June 20 and 21, 1919. Trevisani had been assigned as the paper's special correspondent to investigate and report on the stigmatized mystic of San Giovanni Rotondo. Initially skeptical, thinking Padre Pio might be a "Rasputin," he was won over by the friar's demeanor, and was an eyewitness to a miraculous cure. The recipient of the cure, Pasquale Di Chiara (1881 – 1946), was a functionary of the Ministry of Justice, as chancellor of the prefecture of San Giovanni Rotondo. He was 36 years old at the time, residing at Lucera, about 25 miles from San Giovanni. He had been chancellor at Messina, Sicily, during the great earthquake of 1908 which killed tens of thousands of citizens. For his brave and selfless actions in aiding the wounded and homeless, he merited the official praise of the King's Procurator of the Tribunal of Messina.

In 1918 he received the injury which was subsequently healed by Padre Pio. Pasquale was in Lucera to attend a formal celebration to mark the end of the war between Italy and the Austro-Hungarian Empire, which was concluded by the Armistice of November 3. Civil, military, and religious authorities were present. While descending the stairs of the hotel where the ceremony was held, he took a very serious fall. For three months he was immobilized, and when he finally was permitted to leave his bed, he could only limp along by dragging his leg, painstakingly supported by a cane. When he finally decided to visit Padre Pio at San Giovanni Rotondo, it was not, however, to seek his own cure, as one might think. Instead he sought healing for his three-year old daughter Italia, stricken with infantile paralysis.

The journalist Renato Trevisani obtained the following account from Di Chiara himself of the miraculous occurrence, and included it in his article for the "Mattino." He writes that he was an eyewitness to the prodigy, along with other distinguished personages present at the time who can authenticate it, including the King's Procurator of the Tribunal of Lucera, Dr. Mione; Prefecture Advisor of Sanseverino, Dr. Russo; Dr. Giura; and Vice Magistrate N. Siena.

The headline for the story ran across top of the entire page: "Padre Pio, the 'Saint' of San Giovanni Rotondo." Underneath it ran the sub-heading "works a miracle on the person of the chancellor of the town." The story was in three sections: the Phenomona, Padre Pio, and the Miracles. Available images show only a small part of the complete piece. Pasquale Di Chiara's testimony, as reported in the newspaper, is presented here for the first time in English.

"On November 11, 1918, on the occasion of the conclusion of the Armistice, a small celebration was held at the Hotel Sicilia. Coming down from the hotel, I fell head over heels. After spending three months in bed, under the care of Doctors Merla and Giuva, I was constrained to walk with a cane, dragging my leg, and unable to sustain long walks. At Foggia, I underwent an x-ray examination under Doctor Bucci, which revealed a dislocation.

"I went to the Friary for the first time, together with my wife, to ask Padre Pio for a grace for my little girl of three, Italia, suffering from infantile paralysis. Padre Pio told us to throw away the orthopedic apparatus used on the leg of the child; but my wife, a little wary, did not want to follow the advice. The next day the apparatus broke. My wife told Padre Pio that the child still was not cured, and the friar responded: "It was your fault! Hope, but in God."

"I arrived [another time] at the friary, accompanied by my superiors, who were guests of the city of San Giovanni Rotondo. Seeing me, Padre Pio made a gesture of gentle reproof with his hand, which, however, I did not understand. I remained in the corridor, and in about an hour Padre Pio returned. He stopped before me and said, with his eyes turned upward, a phrase in which I could only make out the word "cane." My friends, Michele Campanile and Benedetto Ventrella, explained to me that Padre Pio had said, "Throw away the cane!"

"He said it a second time, and I let go of the cane, but I remained leaning against a wall. "Man of little faith, go ahead and walk," commanded the Padre. I then experienced a feeling of great warmth in my foot, which in a short time spread throughout my whole body. I now walk normally, without any need of help."

Further details were made known many years later in author Enrico Malatesta's interview with Pasquale Di Chiara's son Umberto, the brother of Italia, who was affected by polio. Following the unexplained breakage of her orthopedic equipment, and the rebuke by Padre Pio to her mother, Italia soon began to walk without requiring any assistance, although with a slight limp. As for Pasquale, he would recall Padre Pio's words: "Man of little faith, go ahead and walk" for the rest of his life. They were spoken with irritation, but in a tone of voice that was at the same time both gentle and gruff. At his command, Pasquale took one step, then two, three and four, and began to cry from joy and emotion. He started to walk faster, and found himself at the feet of Padre Pio, who blessed him with a bright smile.

Sources: *Padre Pio Storia d'Una Vittima*, 1967, Vol. I, pp. 201-202, by Francobaldo Chiocci and Luciano Cirri; and *I Miracoli che Hanno Fatto Santo Padre Pio,* 1998, pp. 57-62, by Enrico Malatesta.

Frank M. Rega

II. A SAINT ON MY BACK

After Cecil's near-death experience, Padre Pio bilocated to hear his confession. Cecil Humphrey-Smith then became the saint's close friend.

In the fall of 1955, Cecil Humphrey-Smith, an Englishman and a convert to the Catholic Church, was a quality-control representative for the H. J. Heinz Company. He was sent to Italy, and was responsible for the tomato fields in the Po Valley. It was his job to determine whether the crops met Heinz' strict standards, and his approval was needed before any fruit or concentrate could be sent to England. That summer, it was hot, with rain and hail, causing lots of problems with the crops. When a farmer notified Heinz that his crop was ready, it had to be inspected immediately for a decision on its acceptability.

With many of his colleagues away, Cecil had to cover a large area of the Valley himself, and on the night of September 24, he returned to his hotel extremely tired after working long days with very little sleep. But then a call came in from a farmer who insisted on having his crop inspected immediately before the rains began again. Reluctantly, he climbed into his car and began a long journey on country roads that been neglected in the ten years since the war had ended. Unfortunately, the rain had resumed and he was forced to reject the crop, to the great dismay of the farmer and his crying wife. He felt very sorry for them, but there was nothing he could do since the unrelenting rain had caused cracks to appear in the tomatoes, with fungus soon to follow, and they would have been rejected if sent ahead.

Driving back late at night and desperate for some much needed sleep, all he wanted to do now was get back to his hotel room. It was then that he had the accident. As he was driving, he dozed off momentarily, and when he suddenly woke up, he accidentally hit the accelerator. As the car shot forward, he saw the headlight of a motorcycle coming towards him; swerving in order to avoid it, he smashed into a bridge, splitting his car in two.

According to Cecil, "At that moment I had what is now termed an 'out-of-body' experience." The fuel tank had landed about 15 feet from the main wreckage, and Cecil, looking down upon the scene, could see his body lying alongside the tank. It was night, on a rural road, in a region where automobiles were few. Eventually a car came along, but it just kept going. The same happened with the next. Finally, a third car approached - by that time Cecil was having a near-death experience, where he entered a long tunnel and was drawn towards a heavenly light. "I knew everything would be all right when I reached that light."

But when the third car passed by, and then stopped and came back, Cecil seemed to find himself back in his body. He heard two men and a woman debate what they should do, finally deciding to drive him themselves to the nearest hospital. As they picked him up, he drifted out of his body again, and saw himself in the back seat of the car, his head resting on a newspaper on the woman's lap. He could see the car all the way to the hospital, "It was if I were traveling just behind and way above it, all the way, going faster and faster."

At the hospital in Piacenza, he became aware that he was being wheeled on a patient trolley along a corridor. He could feel a doctor checking his head and body, and then a sheet was pulled up over his head, and the trolley was pushed into a room. He had no idea how much time had elapsed before he woke up in a hospital bed, after it was discovered he was still alive. His skull was cracked, he had a broken shoulder and collar bone, a cracked vertebra, and ribs, elbow, knee and ankle were broken or badly bruised. "I was in rather a mess."

While he was lying in bed, the door opened and a bearded Franciscan friar entered. He sat down beside Cecil and proceeded to help him, or rather forced him, to make a good confession. "He was pretty brutal at times." When Cecil could not remember something, the priest would tell him what it was, reminding him of such and such a sin in his life. The confession went on and on, and Cecil had to admit that the friar seemed to know things better than he did. No stone was left unturned, his life was thoroughly scoured. "I think subconsciously I was getting a bit cheesed off at the insistence of this priest confessing me." Before he left, the friar administered the last rites to Cecil, consisting of absolution, holy oils, and Holy Communion. Cecil closed his eyes and felt at peace; what he remembered most about this encounter was the priest's most beautiful smile.

The next morning, his close friend and work colleague the Marchese Bernardo Patrizi came by with a local parish priest, who administered Communion again. In the days that followed, Bernardo arranged to have Cecil transferred to a specialized clinic for a time, and from there Bernardo took him to his own palace and estate near Monza. There he was cared for by Patrizi's two daughters, and also by a friend of the family, a princess who was a daughter of Umberto, the last King of Italy.

Eventually he was deemed well enough to return

to work with the Heinz corporation. But he before long he began to have dizzy spells, and would fall asleep at strange times. He started blacking out and had many falls. The worst problems, however, were the excruciating pains in his head, "a pain like a thousand dentist's drills hitting the nerves." Sometimes he would literally bang his head against the wall, smashing up furniture in the process. He was sent to a hospital in London for treatment, which consisted of a few dozen different pills a day. At the hospital he even underwent hypnosis, on the theory that he had subconscious guilt for possibly having killed someone in the auto accident. His statement about the accident under hypnosis was recorded, but he was speaking in Italian! When translated, it turned out to be the same as his original statement.

After further hospitals and years of medical treatments, his old associate Bernardo Patrizi thought it was ridiculous that he should still be suffering, even seven years after the accident. Bernardo asked Cecil to come with him on a journey to meet one of his close friends. Bernardo did not tell him anything about where they were going, but spoke instead about every other possible topic. The trip ended with a harrowing ride up a twisted mountain-side road in the dark. Cecil was in intense pain all the way. Finally they checked into a small hotel called Santa Maria della Grazie, and went straight to bed. They had reached the town of San

Giovanni Rotondo, situated upon the Gargano Mountain.

Very early that morning, Bernardo woke him up and said they were going to Mass. It was snowing and bitterly cold as they trudged up to the church. Although it was still dark out, there was an incredible crowd waiting for the church to open. The doors were finally unbolted, "and then what I can only describe as a 'whoosh' as the crowd surged through and literally ran to fill up the front seats." In his English reserve, Cecil stood aside to let them pass, and as a result he ended up sitting alone near the back of the church. Then an old priest came out to say Mass.

Time seemed to disappear. "From then on all I can say is that I seemed to witness a complete sharing in the Passion, Crucifixion, and Resurrection of Christ. I was transported to the foot of Calvary." Cecil seemed to be in a state of stupor when the Mass ended. Then he realized that Bernardo had found him, and was pulling him towards the sacristy. They entered the room along with a large group of people. He told Bernardo that this was the priest that had confessed him and brought him Communion just after the crash. At one end of the sacristy was a kneeler, where the old priest was making his thanksgiving after Mass. Then he arose and began walking to greet everyone in turn. Cecil was experiencing his usual intense pain, and was disturbed by his recognition of the priest, who warmly embraced

Bernardo. He wondered what Bernardo's relationship with him was.

Bernardo asked Cecil to kneel down, and he said to the priest that this was the Englishman he had told him about. Cecil knelt, and the old priest in a somewhat gruff voice said "*Eh Be. Be,*" while tapping three times on the right side of Cecil's head. "The pain left me immediately." The priest continued walking down the line without looking back. Then he turned to give a final blessing to everyone, and Cecil was transfixed by his eyes. He tearfully rose to his feet, basking in a state of great joy.

In all the years he had known Bernardo, never once had he mentioned that he knew Padre Pio, although he was his spiritual child and close friend. As they left the church and went back down the hill to their hotel, Bernardo began to relate to Cecil about his association with him, and how he was appointed treasurer of his charitable works. While they were at breakfast, one of the friars came dashing in, saying that Padre Pio wanted to see them in his room. They returned to the friary and "chatted" with the saint in his cell. That evening they met with him again in a large drawing room, along with some of the doctors and collaborators of his hospital, La Casa Sollievo della Sofferenza.

As the people arrived, they would kneel to greet

Padre Pio, and kiss his hand. Cecil, with his usual English reserve, bent over and, perhaps because he reminded him of his old grandfather. kissed the Padre on his forehead! Padre Pio took his face in his hands, saying "Bravo, Inglese, Bravo," while patting his cheeks. From then on he always called Cecil "L'Inglese," the Englishman.

They attended these meetings for the next four or five days, and they became engraved in Cecil's memory. As people reported their progress on the Padre's charitable works, there was an atmosphere of warmth and relaxation. With so much being discussed, they seemed to last two or three hours, while in reality they were over in less than half an hour. Padre Pio seemed to have the ability to make time stand still, and to speak to several people at once. He was often joking, yet during the meeting he prayed continuously, his hands constantly turning on the rosary beads. When he would address Cecil, it was as if no one else was there. He seemed to live in a different time, almost beyond time. "I truly believe he had extraordinary abilities, could do many things at one time, and already lived partly outside time."

After the meetings, Padre Pio would participate in night prayers with the community in their internal chapel. The traditional ending of the night prayers was an anthem to the Blessed Mother, the Salve Regina. He always shed tears during this prayer, weeping so copiously that he usually moved the rest of the community to tears as well. He never passed by an image of her without offering a greeting to his Heavenly Mother. While the Vatican Council was in session, someone once asked him if we would ever see women priests. Padre Pio turned on the person quick as a flash, with fire in his eyes. "Would you insult the Mother of God?"

Cecil wrote of these experiences, and much more, in an out-of-print booklet, *A Saint on My Back*. This article is primarily based on a chapter in Jim Gallagher's book *Padre Pio the Pierced Priest*, pp. 155-156, with some input from the Internet. These sources most likely relied on Cecil's booklet.

Frank M. Rega

III. WHEN PHOTOS OF PADRE PIO CAME UP BLANK

In some of the classic biographies of Padre Pio an unusual phenomenon is reported when visitors, pilgrims, or souvenir hunters tried to take his photo: they came up blank. Not always, but there are specific incidents when this was true. John McCaffery recounts one such story in his book, *The Friar of San Giovanni*. During the hot summer months, Padre Pio would occasionally offer Mass outdoors under a portico near the old church. McCaffery was slated to be a server at one of these ceremonies, and his friend Gino was determined to capture the event for posterity. He commissioned a local professional photographer to record the rite, this in spite of the fact that it was well known that Padre Pio was not amenable to being photographed or filmed, especially during his Mass.

As Padre Pio was approaching the outdoor altar, he noticed the photographer and his camera, and told him that he was to take only one or two photos at the

Mass – and the man agreed. The photos were to be ready that afternoon, and McCaffery and Gino eagerly went over to see what the photographer had captured. He was not there, but his sister was, and she informed them that there was nothing to see. Her brother, she said, had tried to be too smart. He had agreed to Padre Pio's conditions, but during the Mass he could not restrain himself, and ended up shooting two complete rolls of film. "They all came out blank." She looked at the two disappointed and irate men as if to say "What else could you expect?" Later that evening McCaffery told the story to Padre Pio's good friend Dr. Sanguinetti, who was instrumental in the founding of Padre Pio's hospital. The Doctor replied that the exact same thing had happened to him – two rolls of film with nothing on them!

Mary Pyle was an American heiress who renounced the material life in order to live near Padre Pio, as a Third Order Franciscan. Interviewed in the 1950's for Maria Winowska's *The True Face of Padre Pio*, Pyle discussed the strange anomaly of the blank photos. She said that for years photographers had been frustrated in their efforts to photograph the saint, sometimes even creeping up on him to take him by surprise, but the negatives always came up blank. On the same roll, there could be magnificent views of landscapes, but on the photos of Padre Pio, there was nothing. Sometimes the shutter refused to move. But pilgrims had such great desire to have a picture of Padre Pio as a souvenir, that "his superiors ordered him to abandon his feud with the cameras." Pyle commented that as a result, "the pictures you will see have been taken quite recently." She added that many years of his life have been irreparably lost to photographers. If it had not been for the ecclesiastical authorities, we should not even have these!

A more recent book, *L'Ultimo Segreto di Padre Pio*, by journalist Enrico Malatesta, uncovers an intriguing new dimension to this phenomenon. Mario De Renzis was a photo-journalist for *Il Tempo*, one of the major daily newspapers of Rome. It was 1960, and at that time the national press was focusing on the stigmatized friar from San Giovanni Rotondo. In an era becoming saturated with materialism, the example given by the humble servant of God constituted a ray of hope for the darkness of modern society. Consequently Mario's editors at *Il Tempo* gave him the assignment to report on and photograph the friary, the crowds, and the beloved friar himself.

The little town of San Giovanni had been portrayed in the media as mecca for those on summer holiday, with tourists regarded as a great source of income. When he arrived at San Giovanni for the first time, he made a quick tour of the area, admiring the church of St. Mary of the Graces, the new hospital "Home for the Relief of Suffering," and noting the many shops and the movements of the people. But when he proceeded to enter the church he was stopped by the ushers, and told that photographers could not be admitted – this would mean the failure of his entire assignment. Fortunately just at that time a number of buses pulled up, and as the pilgrims disembarked and made their way into the church, De Renzis fell in with them, and in this way he slipped inside. Padre Pio was on the altar, and the photographer discretely and with dexterity began to snap his pictures. But he was soon spotted, and the ushers clamored like it was the end of the world. In the ensuring confusion, he made straight for an an exit, and found himself in the garden of the convent.

Noticing a staircase, he clambered up it, entering a little corridor, which led to an open door. It was the entrance to the cell of Padre Pio. In spite of the fact that he had photographed him only a few minutes ago in the church, there he was in flesh and blood, in his room. How was this possible? A healthy person would need at least 15 minutes to get there, and Padre Pio with his painful wounds could only shuffle along slowly. At the time, De Renzis thought no more about it, now that he was in the presence of the saint. He and the Padre "exchanged what is now called in the liturgy the sign of peace," and they shook hands. With his permission, he took a number of pictures of Padre Pio in his cell. The emotions and surprise of this encounter were so strong at the time that the photographer did not fully comprehend what had actually occurred. Padre Pio, the stigmatized priest, had clasped his hand in his own, without any hesitation and minimal discomfort – how could this greeting be possible with a painful and bloody wound in his palm?

As he left the friar's cell, he thought of the marvel that everyone was talking about – bilocation. In view of Padre Pio's extraordinary capabilities, he concluded that he had not been in the presence of the body of Padre Pio, but of his soul, his essence. And physical, bodily pain does not pertain to the soul, which is why Padre Pio was able to "tranquilly shake his hand." His photography assignment accomplished, De Renzis visited the local shops to obtain some souvenirs, before returning to Rome.

At the offices of his newspaper, he developed his photos, and they turned out beautiful: Padre Pio celebrating Mass, the moment of Communion, the great crowds. As for the pictures taken with Padre Pio in his cell, they showed the room clearly, except for one strange thing – there was no Padre Pio visible in the photos! But his assignment at San Giovanni Rotondo was a great overall success, and the newspaper *Il Tempo* sold out at the newsstands.

He never told anyone about what had happened – this particular event was something for him alone, a personal experience of his soul. Even now [around 30 years later] he is filled with nostalgia in thinking about his encounter with the holy friar. Padre Pio, with his extraordinary capabilities, helped him to obtain great satisfaction in his professional field, but much more so in the spiritual. "Now I can say it with greater clarity, my soul is filled with strong emotions that, at the mere memory of the encounter, still make my heart throb."

Thanks to John McCaffery, *The Friar of San Giovanni*, p. 39; Maria Winowska, *The True Face of Padre Pio*, p. 50, Enrico Malatesta, *L'Ultimo Segreto di Padre Pio*, pp. 248-251.

IV. THE LABYRINTH

A Baffling Encounter with Padre Pio.

Was it bilocation, or did he operate outside of time and space?

In the 1950's Gino Lattila was an extremely popular singer in Italy, who had triumphed at the famous Sanremo Music Festival in 1954 with the song "Tutte le mamme." It was not until 1962 that he made his first trip to San Giovanni Rotondo, in order to attend the wedding of his good friend Luciano Rispoli. Luciano's whole family was very devoted to Padre Pio, and his uncle was even a confidant of the saint. Not only were he and his fiancée privileged to be married at the friary, but the celebrant was to be Padre Pio himself.

As for Gino, he was a skeptic and had little sympathy for the stories about the mysterious phenomena associated with him. In fact, he would often laugh at the tales of bilocation, reading of souls, or aromas of perfume. He had attended Jesuit schools, where he received a religious education that was not open to medieval mysticism. Thus, he was not enthusiastic about visiting San Giovanni, even though he would be using his own car to drive the bridegroom there.

The morning after their arrival in the town, Gino, pushed by curiosity, decided to attend Padre Pio's 5:00 am Mass. He was surprised to find that at that early hour the church was packed with the faithful. He listened to the Mass, which was rather long, and was celebrated intently by Padre Pio. Immediately afterwards Gino entered the sacristy along with some of the wedding party, where it was possible to see the Padre close-up and receive his blessing.

Padre Pio was on a kneeler, making his customary thanksgiving after Mass. He was deeply absorbed in prayer; his elbows were resting on a support, and his face was hidden by his hands. Complete silence reigned in the sacristy. There were about fifteen men present, and one of them held a little child by the hand. A long time seemed to pass, and Gino became a little impatient. He knew that Padre Pio's prayer was important, but what about all the people waiting to meet him? Gino started thinking that God would be more pleased if Padre Pio devoted some time to greeting the people.

Suddenly, the little child broke free from his father, and with childhood innocence approached the priest. Perhaps he touched his garments, or maybe he was making some noise. Whatever the reason, Padre Pio turned abruptly and said with a loud voice, "Leave me in peace!" Gino was shocked and scandalized. He had heard that Padre Pio could be gruff, but never imagined he would be that way with children. He thought of the Gospel passage where Jesus said to let the little children come to Him. But this priest instead chases them away! Gino was so angry and upset that, without saying anything to his friends, he trooped out of the sacristy.

For the rest of the day he did nothing but argue about Padre Pio with those of the wedding party. He criticized him for spending so many hours in prayer, while pilgrims were forced to sometimes wait for days and days before seeing him. The relatives of his friend, the groom, who were devotees of the saint, tried to defend him. "The purpose of his mission is the salvation of souls," calmly explained the uncle who was Padre Pio's confidant. "The Padre knows when it is expedient to receive persons or when to make them wait, while they reflect upon their lives. Nothing that happens with Padre Pio is by chance. If he wishes it, he can even arrange to meet you tomorrow."

Those last words struck Gino. The thought, "If he wishes it, he can arrange to meet you tomorrow," constantly turned around in his mind. The words seemed to be menacing, and he was almost fearful. He told himself that he has no desire to meet Padre Pio, and that he has nothing to say to him. But he spent that night in a state of agitation.

The next morning he arose early to prepare for the wedding of his friend Luciano, who had been given a movie camera as a gift. Knowing that Gino was an expert at using one, the groom asked him to film the ceremony. Gino told him he would be very happy to do so. Armed with the camera, Gino drove Luciano from their hotel to the church and parked the car, prepared to film the entire event. As he entered the church, he pondered which was the best place from which to film the entrance of the wedding party. That would be the organ loft at the back of the church.

He looked around for the staircase to reach it. There were two small doors just under the balcony, and he chose to enter the one on the left. Climbing the stairs, he found himself in a corridor, and proceeding further he came to another door. Upon opening it, he was amazed to find himself looking right at Padre Pio! Instantly he recalled that ominous phrase: "If he wishes it, he can arrange to meet you tomorrow." The friar was seated in an old armchair. In the room he could smell the strong odor of fenic acid. [Phenol, a sweet tarry odor that resembles a hospital smell; in Padre Pio lore, it is the aroma that signifies physical and moral sufferings.]

As soon as Padre Pio saw him at the doorway, he glared at him sternly. It was not a look of reproach or rebuke, but it was hard and severe, and penetrated even into the marrow of Gino's bones. He was fearful, but at the same time he felt captivated. He was suffering, yet simultaneously he was happy. He does not know how long the friar fixed on him with his gaze, without saying a word. Perhaps it was a second, perhaps an hour. Finally, with a resounding voice, he asked Gino, "Well, what are you doing here?" Gino responded that he was looking for the organ. The Padre exclaimed, "And here is where you come to look for it?" Then in an imperious tone he commanded, "Get out, get out!".

Gino left the room, closed the door, and rushed away. His face felt all aflame, as if he had been in front of a fire for a long time. He continued on, climbing stairs, going down others, trying to find where the organ was. He began to worry because he was afraid that the spouses-to-be would enter the church before he could film them. At a certain moment he opened another door, and once again, found himself face to face with Padre Pio. "You again?" he said. "But what do you want of me?" However, this time his visage was quite serene, he was almost smiling. Gino excused himself, and withdrew. But this new encounter with Padre Pio had a calming influence. He reflected that if Padre Pio is to celebrate the Mass, and he is still in that room, that means the ceremony has not yet begun. And he resumed his search for the organ.

Since he still could not find it, he descended the stairs in order to go back into the church, but he ended up in another hallway. He opened a door, and for the third time was face to face with Padre Pio. This time he was in the company of a group of children, and was smiling. The children recognized Gino, "It's Gino Latilla the singer on the radio!" The Padre, continuing to smile, said "Oh yes, the Rai, the Rai." [The Rai is Italy's public broadcaster.] He approached Gino, looking him straight in the eye as in their first encounter in his cell, and this time too under his perplexing stare, the singer experienced indescribable sensations. It seemed like his mind was spinning as if someone were stirring it up.

Next Padre Pio raised his hand that was covered by the half-gloves, and struck Gino three times on the head. They were not caresses, but blows, decisive blows, almost punches, as if trying to get him to remember who knows what. He experienced a shudder throughout his entire body. Then with great tenderness Padre Pio said, "Go, and don't ever do anything bad and never be afraid of anyone." With his head clearing, Gino thought of the wedding that he must film, and told the Padre that he had to leave. He walked out, entered another corridor, and finally he found himself in the church.

But no one was there. He looked all around as if lost and he realized that the wedding ceremony must have concluded. It could not be possible. From the time he had begun to look for the organ only five or six minutes had elapsed, while a nuptial Mass has to last at least an hour. Gino felt certain that he had been awake, alert, and in possession of his faculties. Besides, Padre Pio was right here in the friary, he had seen him three times, and there is no way he could have performed the marriage.

Gino walked outside and came upon a relative of his friend Luciano. "But where did you go off to, we were looking everywhere for you," the man said in rebuke. "Weren't you to meet the spouses in their hotel?" Gino replied in the affirmative and asked where they were. The relative answered that the couple were waiting for him until a short while ago, when they left in someone else's car to attend the reception. "What about the wedding?" Gino asked. "Its been over for some time." Gino asked who the celebrant was. "Padre Pio," was the answer.

Thanks to author Renzo Allegri's interviews with Gino Latilla, as reported in his books *I Miracoli di Padre Pio*, pp. 436-440; and *Padre Pio, Il Santo dei Miracoli,* pp. 122-128.

Footnote: I have learned from an Italian magazine, that Gino became a devotee of Padre Pio, who appeared to him many years later when he was partially paralyzed by a stroke and despairing of his future and of his life itself. In this vision he heard Padre Pio tell him he would recover and sing again. After he did recover, Gino would only sing for charity, to fulfill a vow he made after Padre Pio had spoken to him.

V. PADRE PIO'S BILOCATIONS TO IRENE GAETA

How he saved her from a violent attack, and how she saw the Host turn into real flesh. She mentions a book containing the Prophecies of Padre Pio kept by his Friary.

When Irene Gaeta was nine years old and living near Ostia, Italy, she became so traumatized and upset from an attempted rape by a young man that she feared telling anyone about it, not even her parents or the parish priest. She had been lured to the home of an older girl that she knew, where there were a number of other girls and a half-naked man waiting in a bedroom. After she entered, someone locked the door with a key and the young man threw her on the bed. She doesn't remember how, but she got away from under him, falling on the floor. Screaming for help, in her panic she managed to get through the locked door and was able to escape. Afterwards, she lived in fear, afraid to tell about it lest they try to take her again as revenge, and afraid that her father would come after them with a shotgun if she told her parents.

Irene was born in Lanciano to a family with strong Catholic faith and traditions, which was blessed with many priestly and religious vocations. She has always loved the Church, and would give her life for Her, and has always been unconditionally obedient and loyal to priests and pope. Undoubtedly accustomed to prayer even as a child, she received an unexpected visit from a priest some months after her terrifying experience.

It was the evening of June 18, 1946; as she was getting ready to go to sleep for the night, her bedroom became filled with a bright, supernatural light. In that light she could see a priest with a beard, dressed in sacred vestments of white and gold. He appeared to be celebrating Mass, and he blessed Irene with the monstrance. The look in this priest's eyes cut her to the quick, and the emotions she felt in that moment were indescribable. The priest told her to pay careful attention to everything that she sees. Then she saw the host turn into real flesh, and when he raised the chalice, the wine become blood, which overflowed and rained down upon the hands and arms of the priest. As he returned the chalice to the altar, he calmly told Irene not to worry or be afraid.

Following the advice of her grandmother against diabolical deceptions and illusions, she asked him three times who he was. He answered that he was Padre Pio of Pietrelcina, but she had never heard of that town. She told him that she did not know him, and he responded that he is a friar who prays, and one day she will know him. He gave a little tug to her ear, and then showed her what had happened to her not long ago in that bedroom. He said that he was the one who had saved her, opening the door that had been locked securely with a key. She asked him how he could know this event in her life, since not even her parents knew about it. The priest responded "I know everything about you, because ever since you were born, the Eternal Father has entrusted you to my hands. I have saved you and will always save you."

He came closer, now no longer wearing the priestly garments, but dressed as a Franciscan friar. Sitting beside her on her bed, he took her hands in his, telling her not to be afraid, adding: "Look my daughter, this is not a dream, this is reality." As proof, when she gets up in the morning, she is to tell her parents everything about this. "Tell your father to remain calm because all will be well." Her father had recently lost his job and did not know whether he should stay in Rome. Padre Pio told her that in three days he will receive a letter offering work with a salary. "And so that your parents believe what you are saying, tell your mother that I know she had a miscarriage."

Still a child, Irene did not know what a miscarriage was, but her mother confirmed that it had happened, without explaining to her what it meant. Then in thee days a letter arrived from the State Forestry Commission saying that her father had been given a job, and because of his previous good work record and large family, a pension was included. (He had been responsible for the Gardens of the Quirinale, at the service of the King of Italy, until his dethronement by referendum.) Everything was resolved as Padre Pio predicted.

From then on, over the course of many years, Padre Pio helped Irene in all the circumstances of her life. He would often visit her in bilocation, and sometimes she saw him in her dreams. Under his guidance and spiritual fatherhood, she learned to pray to the Eternal Father, the Sacred Heart of Jesus, and to the Heavenly Mother. Sometimes he requested her to pray to save people from the accidental explosion of mines or of unexploded bombs. She approached many people about the Faith, praying with them and inviting them to conversion and confession. He always told her what would happen to her or to her family, no matter if it was good or bad. Since the predictions were not always good news, they began to call her "the little bird of bad tidings." All this time she did not really know who Padre Pio was.

Then one day in the spring of 1957 she was surprised to see his picture on the front page of a newspaper, and she exclaimed to her mother, "This is the friar I always see!" It was only then that she realized that he was still living. She had thought that he must be a saint from the past, since she had been graced with visits from St. Anthony of Padua, St. Gabriel of Our Lady of Sorrows, and the holy souls in Purgatory. The picture in the paper said he was from San Giovanni Rotondo, though she only knew him as Padre Pio of Pietrelcina. As she gazed at the photo it seemed to come to life, taking form before her very eyes. He did not say anything, but looked at her as he did on the first night that he had visited her. She had the feeling he was chiding her for not having come come to see him at his friary.

She wrote to him and he replied. Finally, over two years later, when she was 23, she arrived a San Giovanni Rotondo. It was during the time when Pope John XXIII had placed many restrictions on his ministry. It was extremely difficult to meet with him, and time limitations were placed on his confessions. She entered a confessional, and although Padre Pio was in his friary cell at the time, his face became superimposed over that of the priest who was there. She made her confession to him and he told her many things which she can not repeat. He also gave her some instructions regarding her companion Lucia. He then disappeared, no one else having seen him.

Later he appeared in bilocation to Irene in her hotel room, and told her to return to Rome via Frosinone with her friend Lucia. There was a man dying there who had not seen his daughter for ten years. It was Lucia's father who was dying, and he had asked Our Lady to see his daughter one more time. Irene did as Padre Pio wished, and as they drove to Frosinone, Lucia was amazed since she had never told Irene that her parents lived there. Only a few hours after the reunion between Lucia and her father, he passed on to the Heavenly Father's House, his prayer to Our Lady having been granted.

Irene became an active spiritual daughter of Padre Pio, first going on her own and then organizing several trips to San Giovanni from Rome. As a spiritual father, he did not just look after the souls of his children, but truly and lovingly cared about their whole lives, their activities and their families. Because of her love for the Lord and all that had happened to her, Irene often thought of embracing the monastic religious life. She became a Franciscan Tertiary and embraced the efforts of Catholic Action. When Bishop Ettore Cunial, who was Vicar of Rome at the time of her youth, heard about her experiences with Padre Pio in bilocation, he asked her why she had never told him about it. She answered that until she met him in the flesh, she did not tell anyone except her family because she thought it was a ghost who used to appear to her.

In 1961, on one of her visits to Padre Pio (in the flesh) at his friary, she told him of her wish to enter a convent, and he replied that there is nothing more beautiful than a true vocation. He added, "In three months I will tell you what you must do." When that time arrived he told Irene that he wanted to acquaint her with the elites of the high aristocracy, not because she is to live like them, but to help her understand how poor they really are inside. In a short time, she opened a high fashion atelier as a designer on Rome's Via Frattina. Among her clients were the greatest names of the aristocracy and of the world of entertainment. It that way she was able to help many people return to the love of God and live a life of grace.

Irene eventually married, with Padre Pio's approval of course. She is involved in a host of spiritual and charitable activities, primarily centered on the parish of Vitinia, a Rome suburb. Padre Pio, who has guided her even after his death, asked her to form an association of souls who live the gospel the way he lived it. With a Rule written by the late Father Gerardo Di Flumeri, the vice-postulator of Padre Pio's canonization, the group is called The Disciples of Padre Pio. Initially she was scandalized when Father Gerardo suggested that name, since disciples should be of Jesus. But he told her that "In Padre Pio, Jesus lived! The stones of San Giovanni Rotondo are bathed in the blood of Jesus. If it had not been Jesus in him, he would not have lived more than three days for the blood he was shedding! The Disciples of Padre Pio is also written in the book of his Prophecies." He then gave specific page numbers. Irene asked Father Gerardo to say something more about these Prophecies to her, and he replied "No! It will be given up drop by drop within 100 years, otherwise the world would be upset!"

This article is based on Irene Gaeta's own testimony http://www.idiscepolidipadrepio.it/index.php?lang=en and on her interviews with Jim Gallagher as reported in his excellent book *Padre Pio the Pierced Priest,* pp. 126-135.

VI. UNDER THE PROTECTION OF PADRE PIO

A vein in her brain had burst in four places, her eye was severely damaged, she was comatose, went through a near death experience, and then recovered completely without any consequences.

Teresa Sorrentino lives in a small town nestled in the hills of southern Italy called Cava de' Tirreni, holds three degrees, and is a university teacher. She grew up in a family that was serious about their Catholic faith and of their devotion to St. Francis of Assisi. She is married with two children. In 1972 when she was about 12 years old, she went on a pilgrimage to San Giovanni Rotondo, and developed a great admiration for Padre Pio. Gazing at photos of him, she was struck by the gentle and paternal expression on the face the humble friar. Although she knew little about him at the time, Teresa felt she could understand and empathize with him. From then on, she has always considered him to be her protector. When she learned that he was born on May 25, which was her birthday too, she took this as a special sign that united the two of them.

On a Friday in May of 1998, she was particularly happy, even euphoric. She had learned that she was pregnant with her third child. That morning she began to smell a very sweet perfume. Wondering where it could be coming from, she went from room to room and could sense it wherever she went; but her husband and her mother said they did not notice it. She could even smell it when she was in the car with her husband. The aroma persisted until 2 AM. Teresa did not know at the time that the phenomenon of the perfume often indicated the presence of Padre Pio.

Two days later, she experienced the first signs of a possible spontaneous abortion. She called her doctor, who ordered her to come in for some tests. She was worried, and her thoughts turned to Padre Pio. Another day passed. Then while on the phone with her doctor, she began to feel weak. Her last words to him before she collapsed unconscious onto the floor were "I feel ill." She fell in a dead weight, slamming her head against the telephone receiver – it penetrated her right eye causing a large hematoma and a seriously damaged eyeball.

Teresa was rushed to a nearby hospital, where the gravity of the situation was ascertained – a vein in her brain had burst. But that hospital was not equipped to handle such a case, and she had to be transported to a different one. By the time she arrived there, she was close to death. They did everything possible to save her.

She underwent a cerebral drainage, which only aggravated her condition. She lay in a coma in the intensive care ward, hooked up to IV's, tubes and wires, under the care of the best specialists available. The CT scan revealed an aneurysm, caused by a blood clot from the spontaneous abortion.

Between the aneurysm and the head trauma from her fall, her brain was filling with blood. Her condition was desperate. The coma was considered irreversible, and there was no hope. Even if she did awaken she would be paralyzed, blind in one eye, with disturbances in her speech and thinking; in other words a vegetable.

Yet, while her body was incapacitated, her mind and spirit took flight. She went through that extraordinary experience which many in a coma or near death have reported – a visit to heaven. She felt that she had broken free from her body and had abandoned it. She found herself in that famous dark tunnel, but the darkness was so thick that she became fearful as she traveled through it. Then, at the end of it she found herself immersed in a vibrant, bright light. It was impossible for her to describe the joy and happiness that filled her soul. She comprehended that in that light there were beings, persons, but she could not see anyone. Then, suddenly, she is not sure how, but she recognized her father. She saw him as a very beautiful figure of light, and was able to precisely communicate with him, but not with words.

Her dad had died from throat cancer thirteen years previously. An operation had resulted in a hole in his throat, but here, on the other side, he looked perfect. She asked him why there was no opening in his throat, and he replied that where he is now, there are no physical anomalies of any sort. Then Teresa noticed that near him was another person, a young boy that she knew, who had died at age 18, and was the son of her friend. She marveled at the fact that she was seeing him there; her father said that the boy wanted to give her an urgent and important message to bring back to his family. The boy spoke to her about many things that were later verified.

He told her personal and private details, and explained to her where a certain letter was kept in his house. He described the exact piece of antique furniture and the drawer in which was to be found a maroon colored notebook, within whose pages lay the letter. Upon her return and recovery, Teresa verified that everything he had told her was true. She believes that the encounter with him, since he was not part of her usual circle of friends, had purposely occurred so that she could believe her experience was real. If her father was accompanied by a dead relative, she might have thought that her journey to the afterlife had not actually happened – that it may have been a fantasy or a dream.

Since she considered that the encounter with the boy was real, she also believed that what her father said about her illness was true. He told her that during her horrible misfortune she was protected by Padre Pio. He explained that the perfume she had smelled a few days before entering her coma was that of the saint. Finally, he said that Padre Pio would heal her without any consequences. Then her father told her that she must return to her earthly life. But she replied that should would never want to depart from this place of such peace and immense happiness. However, he insisted, stating that Padre Pio wanted her to return to her family and to give testimony of all she has received. The mention of her family brought back the memory of her two little children, and she realized she must return. Guided by her father and the boy, she reentered the dark tunnel, but this time without any fear.

There is one more incident to relate. Teresa was in a coma for seven days before awakening. When she did, it was in the presence of her mother and a host of doctors and nurses. Shortly before she awoke, her mother had begun to smell the aroma of a very strong perfume. She knew that it signified the presence of Padre Pio. She asked the people in the room if anyone else smelled it, but all they could smell were medicines and carbolic acid. Her mother realized it must be a sign from heaven, since she was the only one that sensed it. So she shouted out with joy that it was the perfume of

Padre Pio, and it meant that her daughter would soon come out of her coma! But the doctors thought she was hysterical, and tried to calm her.

In general, when someone awakens from a coma, they are confused and possibly raving. But about half an hour after her mother first noticed the perfume, Teresa awoke, and she was completely lucid. The doctors were astonished. It was an extraordinary case, one that they had never witnessed. She recognized her mother and cried out in a clear voice "Mamma!" And the date of her return just happened to be "coincidentally" May 25, Padre Pio's birthday.

Teresa was transported to a hospital in Rome, where she underwent two long and difficult operations to repair a vein that had split open in four places. But as Padre Pio had promised, all went well and there have been no consequences. As for her damaged right eye, it has mysteriously recovered completely, although the oculists had told her she would lose half of her vision in it. Shortly after her discharge, she resumed her university studies. According to the doctors, her recovery is a "miracle of nature," but she knows she owes everything to Padre Pio. She is a member of a Padre Pio prayer group, and dedicates every moment of her free time to him, giving her testimony.

Based on an article by Renzo Allegri, in *Padre Pio Il Santo de Miracoli,* pp. 41-45.

VII. THE CURE THAT SHOULD NOT BE

After a terrible accident, he was unable to bend his left knee, until he knelt in Padre Pio's confessional. But after the miraculous cure, the medical impediment to bending his knee still existed!

This is an example of a cure which should not be. Giuseppe Canaponi suffered from fibrous ankylosis, the stiffening of the knee due to the presence of fibrous bands around the bones forming the joint, and his left leg was completely rigid. The clinical examinations and tests after the cure showed that the physical condition which caused the infirmity continued to persist. There are many reports of the miraculous cure of Mr. Canaponi in the Padre Pio literature, and they differ in some of the particulars. Therefore, I have written the following from the earliest account I have been able to discover.

It is from an interview with journalist Carlo Trabucco, published May 17, 1951 in a Catholic newspaper of Bologna. He interviewed the railroad worker Giuseppe Canaponi at San Giovanni Rotondo, near Padre Pio's friary. He describes Giuseppe as 38 years old, of average height, with a smiling and pleasing face. At first he was a little embarrassed to tell his story, and did not know how to begin.

Canaponi: "You see how I am walking?"

Trabucco: "I see it."

Canaponi: "Do you know where I am from?"

Trabucco: "Tuscany, no doubt."

Canaponi: "Have you heard about it?"

Trabucco: "A little."

Trabucco writes: This was just small talk, while he sought to gather his thoughts and present them in a certain order.

Canaponi: "I want to tell you about my adventure. You see this left leg? Three years ago it was a rigid stump, and now it is like a new leg. I received it anew back there, in the sacristy. How it happened I don't know. It is necessary that I explain to you how I recovered this left leg, but first let me tell you how I lost it. At Sarteano, my home town that is near Chiusi, a truck on June 26, 1946, broke the femur of my left leg."

Trabucco writes: Saying this, he rolled up his trousers and showed me scars that provoked horror.

Canaponi: "I made the rounds of the hospitals in the area, Sarteano, Chiusi, Montepulciano, Siena and then Rizzoli in Bologna. It was useless. The conclusion you can read here in this original declaration of a hospital release in April, 1951. Here is what it says: 'This is to certify that Mr. Giuseppe Canaponi was hospitalized in this clinic in 1948 for *anchilosi rifrosa* [stiffness, rigidity] of his left knee due to a fracture of the femur. All the therapies, medical and physical, that were tried in order to force articulation under general anesthesia, did not work. Instead, these maneuvers succeeded in re-fracturing the femur. He was dismissed with his knee as rigid as it was upon his admittance.' Signed by the Director, Giuntini. "Have you read this? Did you understand?"

Trabucco: "I believe so. Knee is rigid, that is, it cannot be bent. And now I see that you can walk."

Canaponi: "Walk? I run, I jump . . . you are looking at a person reborn. Before, I could not take it anymore. I blasphemed, cursed – my wife did not know what to do. I had some scary crises, during which I became like a beast. Then I would calm down and repent, until the next time. The leg caused me tremendous torture. Enduring great pain, I could take only a few steps using two crutches. My wife wanted me to go see Padre Pio. But I rebelled, and inveighed against him, but not knowing what else to do I relented. I went to see him accompanied by my wife and my son. In my condition it was not a pleasant journey."

"On the afternoon of December 28, 1948 I was in the sacristy for my confession to Padre Pio. He said to me: "You blaspheme much, you curse everyone, you are restless." I replied, "Yes Padre, it is true. It was the sufferings, the long illness, the injections that had changed me." The Padre went on: "However, afterwards you repented, went into your room and prayed." I said to myself, "This is strange, he knows everything, he is telling me my confession. I said, "Padre, pray that the Lord removes from me this brutal defect." He replied, "You must be a strong person, otherwise it would be useless for the Lord to give you the grace."

"Only in that moment did I realize that I was kneeling down, and I said to myself that I have already received the grace because I have bent my knee that for three years has been immobile! I rose up, taking my crutches, and instead of using them to support me, I carried them in my arms. With my son I went into the church where my wife looked at me with amazement upon seeing me walk. "Yes, it is true," I said. "It seems to me that in the sacristy I had even knelt." My wife did not want to believe this, and my son said, "Yes, Papa, I saw it, you were on your knees."

"As if dreaming we returned to the hotel, and in the room I took a pillow, laid it on the floor, and went down on my knees. It was true. It was true. The next morning I went to Padre Pio to thank him for the grace, but he told me: "It was not I who gave you the grace. Thank the Lord, only the Lord."

Trabucco writes: And that was the "adventure" of Giuseppe Canaponi. Then I asked him "And the doctors?"

Canaponi: "When I returned to Sarteano everyone was astonished, friends and enemies. The curious thing is that this grace caused enmity among some who were my friends. Meanwhile, the railroad was going on with the process to have me discharged and sent home. In order to stop the proceedings, I asked for a visit at Florence from the Railroad Inspector. It was granted and I made known to professor Prosperi what had happened. He read and re-read what was in the hospital records and exclaimed that according to these documents, I would never be able to bend my knee. I told him that for me it is otherwise. He said that he sees it, and I am correct and not the records, because I can walk. Therefore, I remained working at the railroad and returned to my usual post at the station in Chiusi. Now, every time that I can, I travel to San Giovanni Rotondo, because here is where I recovered my health and my peace of soul."

In a further interview, years later, conducted by Renzo Allegri, Canaponi said that when he and his family arrived back home in Sarteano, it was New Years Eve. There was a celebration and dance at a local venue, and he and his wife decided to attend. When he entered, walking normally, the room became quiet as a tomb. Everyone had known about his condition, and that he could not take a step on his own, and they also knew that he had been to see Padre Pio. The people from that area were almost all communists, thus they were not open to believing in miracles. Seeing that he was cured, they were embarrassed. But he embraced his wife, and they began to dance. Everyone stepped aside, but then after a few minutes the people began to applaud. They danced for over two hours.

In the following days, he returned to the clinic at Siena, and the doctors were astonished. First of all, just in seeing him walk. And then, because the x-rays of his knee showed that nothing had changed. The *anchilosi rifrosa* was still present, and they said that it is not possible that he could be walking. Later, Professor Giuntini presented his case in Rome at a medical congress. There Canaponi was examined by various specialists, who marveled at his case.

Ultimately, Giuntini released a formal document, stamped and signed "University of Siena, Orthopedic Clinic, Director Leopoldo Giuntini." The last sentence reads "We therefore have reason to believe that the sudden recovery of the articular movement, in the case of Mr. Canaponi, constitutes an extraordinary event that can not find, within the limits of current scientific knowledge, a logical explanation."

Before seeing Padre Pio, Giuseppe had been declared a permanent invalid. Since the physical cause of his disability was still present even after the miracle, the doctors continue to confirm his status as an invalid. "Even today, for science and for the state, I am an invalid: I cannot walk; and yet, as you see, I walk in a perfect manner."

Trabucco interview based on F. Chiocci and L. Cirri, *Padre Pio Storia D'una Vittima*, pp. 667-669. Also, Renzo Allegri, *Padre Pio Il Santo de Miracoli*, pp. 344-349.

Frank M. Rega

VIII. HIS TWELVE APOSTLES

Unlike those of Jesus, Padre Pio's were all women.

Nina Campanile was one of the first of Padre Pio's spiritual daughters, not just in the order of time, but also in the height of her spirituality. Nina was a primary school teacher in San Giovanni Rotondo. She first met the Padre on October 5, 1916, only one month after he was assigned to the friary of Our Lady of Graces at San Giovanni. Although he had just arrived, and the stigmata were not to appear for another two years, his reputation for holiness was already spreading in the Puglia region of southern Italy.

World War One was raging, and Nina's younger brother had recently died at the front. Their mother was worried about his eternal fate, so she asked Nina to visit the "holy monk" to ask if he was saved. She did so, and the reply of the Padre was: "If the mercy of God depended on what you think, all men would be in hell. He is saved, yes, and in need of prayers." In her diary, she wrote that her first impression of him was that he was entirely a supernatural being, "with a halo around his head," because at that time she did not understand that before saints can be illuminated by the light of paradise, they first had to be truly human.

Once she had met him, she found it difficult to be away from his presence, and that initial meeting proved to be the beginning of many others, either in person or by letter, through which Padre Pio provided for her spiritual direction. He told her that he understood from their first encounter, that the Lord had sent her to him, and that much work would be required to form her soul in God. About that visit, Nina wrote: "He penetrated to the depths my soul, without my having spoken, such that I felt ashamed to be in his presence, and I did not dare to raise my eyes to look up at him, so much was the confusion that I felt."

Twice a week, Thursday and Sunday, and often on other days, Nina came to see Padre Pio along with some of her teacher colleagues and other spiritual daughters. Conferences took place in the guest parlor in an informal, friendly atmosphere, where he taught the way of perfection, and spoke about the gospel. They would ask him about things they did not understand, and with paternal gentleness, he would resolve their difficulties and doubts, enlightening their minds.

He told Nina that it was his intention to form a few, good souls, so that they in turn would be the seeds sown in the bosom of the of the people. Whenever he talked to them one-on-one in private, he would not only be interested in their spiritual growth, but also showed an interest in their families, as if he were himself a family member wanting to know what was happening to his loved ones. If one of them were sick, he would inform them of any steps to be taken. "In this way this exquisite conquistador of souls captivated our faith, such that we manifested to him the most intimate fibers of our consciences; he sifted and directed our sentiments and our spirits, steering them towards the supreme ideal."

Nina writes that there were twelve women who attended Padre Pio's conferences. In her memoirs she lists them as Rachelina Russo, the Ventrella sisters, Giovanna and Lucia Fiorentino, Lucia Campanile [Nina's sister], Maria and Antonietta Pompilio, Maria Ricciardi, Filomena Fini, and Maddalena Cascavilia. Padre Pio said that "Here it is not a question of personal acceptance. Souls are attracted as the Lord disposes."

From the very first meetings, he taught that their spiritual progress hinged upon five basics. These were: weekly confession; daily Communion; spiritual reading; meditation; and nightly examination of conscience. At whatever the cost, he did not want them to neglect daily Communion, unless they had committed a mortal sin. In order to allay any doubts, he listened to all of their frequent fears and scruples about approaching the altar. He told them that they should abstain from Holy Communion only if they knew for certain they had sinned mortally. In this way he triumphed over their fears. Following the example of his twelve spiritual daughters, in a very short time the practice of daily Communion diffused itself throughout San Giovanni Rotondo.

But the teaching of Padre Pio was not simply catechetical, he used various means to make them understand and penetrate the truth. In her initial years under the Padre's tutelage, he treated Nina in an exceptional way in comparison to the others – he treated her as if she were a little child. He often gave her very pretty holy cards and sacred objects, and gave her all the candy and sweets that his devotees had personally given to him. In her spiritual blindness, Nina thought that these gifts were a sign of her special predilection in the eyes of God and of the Padre. However, as time went on, she began to think about the poverty of Saint Francis of Assisi, yet here she was eating sweets. She mentioned this to Padre Pio, who immediately responded, "That is why I don't eat them, and give them to you instead." She replied, "Am I not also a daughter of St. Francis, so then why do you give them to me?" He answered in jest, "You are not the daughter of St. Francis [San Francesco], but of your dad, Don Francesco." And they both laughed. But the wisdom of this little joke reached into her heart. And she considered it often, especially when the daughter of Don Francesco, who wished to be the daughter of St.

Francis, had a great desire for sweets and candy.

God was in him in a supernatural manner the way that natural things are in us, and Nina cited many facts which demonstrated it. During the first year under her direction by the Padre, her mother was stricken with a very high fever. The doctors diagnosed double pneumonia, and the family was very concerned. When Padre Pio met with Nina, he asked how her mother was doing. She told him that the doctors were prescribing certain treatments for the pneumonia, including eight leeches [bloodsuckers – *sanguisughe*]. Padre Pio exclaimed that her illness was actually a severe case of malaria. A short time later, the diagnosis that Padre Pio had discerned supernaturally, was confirmed.

In February 1918 her sister had a terrible fall from a great height; she was in severe pain and lost consciousness. A doctor was urgently summoned, and he diagnosed that she had suffered serious internal bruises and her kidneys had become displaced – she would die before the night was over. Nina ran over to the friary through sleet and snow, to find Padre Pio, and he reassured her that "This is just God accosting her, she will soon be healed." But that evening her sister was still lying unconscious on her bed. Nina called out to her loudly, shook her, even pinched her, but there was no response. All of a sudden the face of Nina's friend, who was also present, began to pale, as she announced, "The Padre is here." It was bilocation.

Nina was stupefied, never having experienced anything like it before. "But the Padre is here?" she asked. "Yes, he is here in spirit." "How is he dressed?" "Like a monk." "If I reach out to touch him, can I feel anything? "No, because it is his spirit. See? He has come near your sister and said 'poor girl.' " After about ten minutes her friend said, "Now, he has gone away." Nina wanted to verify the reality of this event, and carefully noted that the time was 8:00 pm. She approached her sister's bedside, and once again called out to her. To Nina's surprise, she responded with a profound sigh, and said she was feeling much better. The next day Nina went to the friary, and when she saw the Padre she asked him point blank, "Padre, what time did you come to the house last night to see my sister?" "Around eight o'clock," he replied. The proof was evident, and her sister was cured.

Nina's nephew was a medic serving on a hospital ship, and one day she heard that the ship was bombed. Fearful, she immediately approached the Padre and asked him about her nephew. He replied without hesitation, "Be calm, he was in port and not on the ship." Later, she learned that this was in fact the case. Padre Pio could not have learned that her brother was safe by normal means, since she had asked him as soon as news came of the bombing.

Nina wrote that the stormy times in which we live have need of a "divinized being" on earth to give an example, comfort, sustain, and above all to support us through the raging and furious storms, to insure that if the body is lost, the soul will not be. The life of Padre Pio, like that of the Divine Master, is one of total sacrifice. He eats little, and sleeps even less. He prays, works, suffers. Forgetting himself, his life is dedicated to the cause of souls; he is open to everyone. He said, "If you do good to those who deserve it, what merit is there? It is necessary to know how to treat with the bad and with the good, in order to draw out the best in the one and in the other."

Based primarily on Enrico Malatesta's *La Vera Storia di Padre Pio*, pp. 136-143. Additional information from *Letters* of Padre Pio, Vol III, pp. 949-950.

Frank M. Rega

IX. HE SHUFFLED THERE ON HIS STIGMATIZED FEET

The night Padre Pio left his monastery and walked to the home of a dying man.

Dr. Francesco Ricciardi, a practicing physician for many years at San Giovanni Rotondo, had always manifested a certain aversion towards Padre Pio. The doctor was a man with a very frank and sincere character, honest to the point of being scrupulous. A tireless scholar, he thought his studies could not admit of the supernatural. God was a utopia. Padre Pio was a conventionalism created only for the ignorant; science, only it, was an infallible dogma, and only in that did he believe.

He supported the attacks that Padre Pio's own archbishop, Mons. Pasquale Gagliardi, launched against him. He freely took part in the petty meetings that were organized in the town in order to express disapproval of the work of the priests, and to defame the very person of the humble friar, often also to launch insults and blasphemies in his direction. And the good priest of God, although knowing all about it, never spoke one word of blame against the wickedness that so cruelly offended him in the most noble of his prerogatives – the priesthood.

Ricciardi had not approached the confessional in thirty years, and had never desired to bow down his white-haired pate before an image of Christ or the Virgin Mary. But the "Dies irae" would arrive even for him. Padre Pio would be there at the gate, not in order to punish, nor to reprimand, but to bestow instead the holiest and unexpected of conversions.

In the fall of 1928, the doctor fell sick. A terrible disease had undermined his very existence, and it was so serious that it seemed to be carrying him to the tomb. It was stomach cancer, causing his strong constitution to wither from day to day. His doctor, Francesco Giuva, assisted by colleagues Dr. Angelo Maria Merla, Dr. Tomasso Morcaldi, Dr. Capuano Matteo, Dr. Antonio Mauricelli, were all of the opinion that he would die. "I am dying, Giuva," murmured Dr. Ricciardi to his colleague, "It is finished."

From Foggia, Naples and many parts, the doctors arrived at San Giovanni Rotondo, and each could do nothing but confirm the diagnosis of their colleagues; only Dr. Merla thought that instead of stomach cancer it might be acute gastritis [gastrite flemmonosa.] All treatments were attempted, including radiation, but nothing availed to stop the disease. Dr. Ricciardi was dying little by little.

Numerous priests alternately approached him, all presenting to him thoughts of peace, of love, of repentance. But he refused them all, affirming that he intended to die as he had lived. A friend of the family thought of Padre Pio. "Only he, only he," she said, "can work a miracle."

In December, Don Giuseppe Principe, parish priest of the town, who was the doctor's personal friend, was called to administer the last rites, while the patient was still conscious. But as soon as he saw the priest he chased him away with unheard-of fury, saying, "I do not want a priest, I don't want anyone." He even threw a slipper at him from his bedside. In a moment of exasperation he shouted at the unfortunate man, "No one can hear my confession, only Padre Pio, whom I have so much offended, could I confess to today. But he can not come over here, and so I prefer to die as I am."

Outside the wind howled frightfully, a heavy sleet penetrated the clothing, chilling even the hearts of the good countrymen who were gathering near his home. They were already crying over the respected doctor, who so lovingly for many years had taken care of them. He was very popular, he often tended the sick for nothing, and was generous-hearted.

The end was near. The death rattle was already fading, and the body was beginning to give out the odor characteristic of death, when the doctor who rebelled against the laws of God, saw appear in the doorway the humble Franciscan friar – Padre Pio had been alerted and asked to hasten to the bed of the dying man, with pleas that he alone could give a new soul to God.

That evening a pious person had made his way to the monastery of the friar who bore the wounds of Christ, and told him what was occurring. Padre Pio wished to leave immediately, but he had to obtain permission from the Guardian, Padre Raffaele. He was at first reluctant, but he relented and even accompanied Padre Pio to the sick man's home. It had been ten years since the Padre had left the confines of the friary of St. Mary of the Graces. The superior ecclesiastical authorities, in order to avoid fanaticism, had imposed upon him certain determinate restrictions, which only had the effect of greatly increasing the flames of love for him.

No authors give the actual location of Dr. Ricciardi's home. Maria Winowska writes it was only a "few yards" from the convent, and that Padre Pio "shuffled on his martyred feet to see the doctor." It must have been a short distance from the monastery, perhaps down the main road from the friary, the Viale

Cappuccini. Alberto Del Fante, who was the first to write about the incident, informs us that the person who went to fetch the Padre, over the resistance of Dr. Ricciardi, was Dr. Angelo Maria Merla, who at one time was also an atheist. "He told me himself in February of 1931 that instead he believes in God and is a good Catholic and spiritual son of Padre Pio."

Notwithstanding the late hour, the bad weather, and the distance to be covered, Padre Pio "shuffled" down the road, desiring only to reach the bedside of the poor sick man. He took with him from the little Chapel of Santa Maria delle Grazie, a consecrated Host and holy oils, and along with these two precious helps from heaven, was Padre Raffaele. As he approached the house, he was recognized by passers-by, who gathered around him and accompanied him to the place where Dr. Ricciardi lived, joining those that were already in front of the home praying for his conversion and healing.

While Padre Pio continued towards the bedside of the sick man, the growing crowd of people who had heard of what was happening began kneeling along the roadway by the house, now lovingly visited by Lord present in the Host. They were crying and praying prayers of peace, consolation, and love. All the while, large flakes of snow were falling, as some manna from heaven coming to bless the auspicious event that was to take place in the humble room of the dying man.

Padre Pio reached the bedside of Ricciardi, and embraced him with a smile, as proof of his forgiveness. As soon as the doctor saw the priest, he seemed to experience an infinite wellbeing. The atheist was conquered. The atheist bowed that head which he had never bowed, the atheist joined his hands, made the sign of the cross, and after confessing, received the Holy Eucharist and Extreme Unction from the stigmatized hands of the Padre of Pietrelcina. God entered into him, God, who can not abandon and does not abandon. The smell of death was overcome by the perfume that emanated from Padre Pio, the impure soul became pure, and the lips that for thirty years only spoke empty words, were now thanking God.

Rev. Bernard Ruffin reports that he whispered to Padre Pio saying, "Father bless me one more time. There is no more hope for me, and in a little while I will be dead, and so I want to leave the world with your pardon and another blessing from you." But the good Padre responded: "Your soul is healed, and soon your body will be healed as well. You will go to the friary and repay the visit that I have made this evening." After having once again kissed and blessed him, the Padre left the house in order to walk back to his friary.

Outside of the home of the doctor, the people, defying the wind and snow, waited for the miracle. And the miracle arrived! Padre Pio once again chased away death and gave to the Divine Lord a new soul. Dr.

Ricciardi survived, happy to have found the light, the spiritual light, that illuminated his white hairs. All signs of the cancer were gone in three days, and Dr. Ricciardi did in fact come to the friary church to thank God and Padre Pio.

The renowned doctor, in that unforgettable day, after his close contact with the humble herald of heaven, was cured of a very serious double infirmity: that of his soul, because from that moment onward he continued to live devoted and thankful to the one who was so good to him – and that of his body, because he was cured of his physical malady. He was able live for almost another four years, doing good works and most importantly thanking the Lord, who had forgotten the affronts He had received, and had given him back both spiritual and material life. He died in June of 1932 at the age of 71.

This was perhaps, according to Dr. Giorgio Festa, the one and only time Padre Pio, driven by love and the desire to do good, left his sanctuary of peace and prayer. [Other than to vote.] Dr. Festa reported that those who had been present at the event, in remembering what had occurred as they told him about it, had tears in their eyes from the intense emotion that had reawakened in their hearts.

Comment of Alberto Del Fante: "Almost all of these doctors mentioned are still alive. I do not cite facts from Mr. X or Mr. Y, but facts verifiable by all who desire to touch with their hands or see with their eyes, or hear with their own ears." He quotes the Gospel of St. John (3: 20-21). "For every one that doth evil hateth the light, and cometh not to the light, that his works may not be reproved. But he that doth truth, cometh to the light, that his works may be made manifest, because they are done in God."

Translated freely from two historical sources for Padre Pio: Alberto Del Fante, *Per La Storia* VI Edition, 1948 pp. 312-314; and Dr. Giorgio Festa, *Misteri di Scienza e Luci di Fede,* 1949 pp. 244-246; Also C. Bernard Ruffin *Padre Pio the True Story*, 1991 pp. 224-226, 340; and Maria Winowska, *The True Face of Padre Pio,* 1955, pp. 140-141.

X. ANATOMY OF A CONVERSION

Worldly, cosmopolitan, elegant, she had no time for the things of God . . . until she met Padre Pio.

Luisa Vairo was born into a wealthy family, which zealously strove to cater to her every whim. She grew up to be highly cultivated and intelligent, but could find neither in the books that she read nor in the luxuries of life, any enjoyments that really gave her true satisfaction. She was an independent person, who shone in high social circles, yet her refined, elegant tastes were never totally fulfilled. Consequently, she was always looking for something new, unexpected, and different. Although beautiful, clever and rich, all the pleasures and sensations that she sought after left her with more disgust than joy. Unfortunately, her materialistic life made Luisa insensible and even prejudiced against any thought of a hereafter, and she scoffed at anyone who spoke to her of God. In fact, she was vehemently anti-clerical.

One day in the mid 1920's, one of her circle of friends, a gentleman whom she knew very well, departed from London, where Luisa was then living, and headed for Rome on a pleasure trip. While in the Eternal City, this man heard about a monk named Padre Pio, and impelled by a desire to meet him, he traveled to San Giovanni Rotondo. When he returned to London after encountering the saint, he was like a new person, almost opposite to what he was before. When his group of friends began talking in a bawdy way, he expressed his disapproval, manifesting that he no longer thought of such things the way he used to.

Vairo and her companions, knowing that he had been to Rome, began to mock him: "Now that you have been to Rome, you want to be a monk!" But he replied calmly and firmly, "I have not become a monk, but I have completely changed, and the person who caused this change is in fact a monk." They would not let him continue speaking, drowning him out with their mockeries and laughter. But he remained calm, and their shouting failed to disturb him. Finally they desisted, and asked him to tell his story. He answered: "I myself will tell you nothing, you go and see for yourselves."

But later on he told Luisa about San Giovanni and Padre Pio, and this aroused in her an ardent curiosity and a desire to visit this Padre. Ever the lover of something new and unexpected, she soon undertook the journey to visit the modest hermitage where Padre Pio lived. Upon her arrival, she was immediately disgusted by the town, which was then very primitive, quite unlike what it was eventually to become. Used to cosmopolitan society, fancy palazzi and luxurious hotels, she made up her mind to return home immediately after encountering Padre Pio.

However, as she clambered up the rugged, and at that time unpaved, trail that led towards the convent, she started to think about and experience strange new sentiments and feelings that she had never before known. Perhaps it was the tiny birds flying among the branches of the budding almond trees, or the murmur of distant waters, or the bright azure sky of "Bella Italia," or the song of a shepherd with his sheep. The sad reality of her life appeared before her mind, as she thought of the life that she had lived without accomplishing anything. She felt a sense almost of rebellion against herself for having hearkened to the world of appearances instead of listening to her own heart. Reaching the top of the Patariello, the hillock upon which stood the bare, plain monastery and chapel of Our Lady of Graces, a wave of melancholy and then one of infinite sweetness arose within her. She was overwhelmed by the combination of all these new sensations along with the thought of actually encountering the Padre who had changed her friend's life – the anticipation of coming before the stigmatic who was said to see and know everything about one's soul!

Arriving at the threshold of the little church, she found herself trembling and fearful, yet hopeful. But as she entered she could not hold back her loud sobs and tears, which fell in torrents from the depths of her soul, overflowing from the sorrowful pains she felt within herself. She would later state: "I can only say that in that church I felt the ice in my heart melting." Some women who were nearby in the sacristy heard her bitter sobs, and hurried towards her, followed by Padre Pio himself. As soon as he saw Luisa, and before she could say a word he said to her: "Be calm, Signora, be calm! The mercy of God is infinite, and Jesus died on the cross for sinners." She noticed at once an exceptional brightness about him, and she began to feel more tranquil. The other women did not know the hidden reasons for her tears, but they knew enough to let her alone with the Padre.

She asked him to hear her confession, but told him that she would not know what to say or to do. He replied that this was not the time for it. She should remain calm and come back at three o'clock, when he would confess her. If she did not know what to say, he would say it for her. She went into the church and tried to make an examination of conscience, but in fact she did not recall how to, since she had been away from the sacraments for so many years. And besides, she could not remember all of the many sins she had committed.

She returned at the appointed time that

afternoon for her confession a little calmer, but she was still rent with tears and sobs, which made her unable to even speak to him. However, Padre Pio himself began by describing all the varied and diverse periods of her life, her adventures and vicissitudes, and pointed out the grave errors she had committed, and how they had kept her far away from God. When he finished enumerating her sins, he asked Luisa if she could recall anything else that should be confessed. In her heart she felt two distinct impulses. One said that she should confess a certain other sin, even though Padre Pio had not mentioned it, otherwise the entire confession would be invalid. But another voice within her said that it is not necessary to tell it, since Padre Pio would have listed it with the others if it were important. Fortunately, Luisa followed the good impulse, and confessed to him the sin that had been omitted. Padre Pio replied, "Finally . . . this is what I was waiting for." And he gave her absolution.

She left the chapel filled with happiness, experiencing for the first time the joy and the peace that she had vainly tried to capture through her worldly pursuits. She later said that if she had been keeping a daily journal all of her life, the description of her sins would not have been as exact as Padre Pio's account of them, since he had not overlooked even the smallest fault.

Now desirous of completely renewing her life,

she remained at San Giovanni Rotondo, daily making the trek to the convent along with other devotees of the Padre, and the visiting pilgrims. She took up residence in the home of the Fiorentino sisters, who were among his very first spiritual daughters. They instructed her in the steps of the spiritual life, and she spent the greater part of her days at the church. She commenced to undertake penitences, privations, and mortifications not only for herself, but also for the conversion of her son, who was assigned to a ship in the Navy.

The fancy and elegant shoes from Paris and Rome that she once wore had become an odious memory. One day, when the weather was so bad it kept many away from going to the church, she made up her mind to walk there on her bare feet, as an act of mortification. The wind was howling, and the sleet penetrating her clothing felt like piercing thorns, but none of this deterred her. Exhausted, frozen, soaked to her bones, she reached the convent hardly able to stand on her feet. They had become swollen and bloody from plodding up the stony, rugged trail.

As she crossed the threshold of the Church, she fell in a faint, and was taken into the sacristy. The icy water dripped down from her garments, beginning to melt once she was indoors. As soon as he saw her, Padre Pio told her that she was too rash in doing such penance. "Our body is like a donkey that must be disciplined, but not too severely, otherwise it will collapse and be unable to carry us." Then he placed his hand on her shoulder, saying: "This water does not wet." And immediately her clothes were completely dry!

But nothing could deter Luisa from her penances, especially because of her son. Each time she spoke of him to the Padre, he would tell her to keep praying, because someday he too would see the light. She often wrote to her son about her conversion, but he did not believe it was genuine. Simply in order to please her he promised to come to San Giovanni Rotondo some day. But Luisa felt no peace in thinking that her worldly life had given him a bad example. Then after many months of penance at St. Mary of the Graces, a visitor brought with him some newspapers from England. Leafing through them in the square in front of the church, she let out a scream that was heard by everyone inside. She had read that his ship had sunk at sea, and over a dozen men had perished – but their names were not given.

Many rushed out from the church in order to calm her. When Padre Pio arrived, she told him that she feared her son was dead. He asked her "Who told you he has died to cause you such desperation?" She replied, "Can you assure me he is alive?" Padre Pio looked at Luisa, who was crying buckets, and then he raised his eyes heavenward. After a few moments he said: "Thank the Lord, your son is alive!" Padre Pio told her where he was staying, even stating the exact address. All the onlookers marveled.

Luisa Vairo wrote a letter to her son, explaining how Padre Pio had given her the address, and begging him to come and give thanks for his escape from danger. Finally convinced, he obtained leave to come to San Giovanni for a day. His mother urged him to go to confession, and to fast in order to receive Communion. He promised her he would fast, but on the way to the church he stopped for a little snack of some eggs and grapes. Arriving at the sacristy where his mother awaited him, he was introduced to Padre Pio. The saint looked at him and said with a knowing smile: "What a rogue, what a liar!" The man was insulted, and asked Padre Pio, who had never met him before, why he was saying these things to him. He replied, "Are you going to insist to your mother that you have been fasting? What about those two eggs and those grapes that you have eaten?" Luisa's son became greatly disturbed, and then went down on his knees before the Padre, entreating him: "Padre, pardon me. I believe!"

This article is based on accounts in Alberto Del Fante's *Per La Storia*, pp. 279-288, and on *Padre Pio Storia D'una Vittima*, by Francobaldo Chiocci and Luciano Cirri, pp. 630-632.

XI. HE WANTED TO KICK PADRE PIO

Alfredo was a practicing Catholic, but he did not give any special credence to the saintliness of Padre Pio. And he felt it was not a sin to feel that way since for him a saint was someone that the church had proclaimed as such, and that could not happen for a very long time. After all, it was 1950 and Padre Pio was still alive and well. But Alfredo did want to make a visit to San Giovanni Rotondo to find out more about this friar, if for no other reason than to satisfy his curiosity.

He carefully planned his trip to occur at a time when he thought there would be few visitors to the friary, so that he would have more time to observe the priest that everyone was talking about. Unfortunately for him, he reasoned that a good time to visit would be on November 2, All Souls Day, in Italian *il Giorno dei Morti,* the Day of the Dead. Alfredo had no idea that Padre Pio was already famous for his intercession for the souls in Purgatory, and that crowds of visitors and petitioners would converge on the tiny friary that day.

He took the train from his home in Potenza to Foggia, and the bus from there to San Giovanni was so packed that he was forced to stand in the aisle for the entire trip up the Gargano mountain. Then after he finally reached the church, he learned that he needed to make a reservation to confess to Padre Pio, and had to wait a week for his turn to arrive. In the meantime Alfredo, being resourceful, decided to at least be present in the sacristy when Padre Pio confessed the men, and also when the priest returned to the sacristy in the early evening to prepare for Vespers – evening prayer.

An hour after confessions were over, Padre Pio descended from his cell to enter the sacristy prior to the Vespers service. By that time, only a few men were present and Alfredo had a good opportunity to get close to the friar and observe him clearly. Yet, even after he came to know Padre Pio well in the years to come, he still does not really know how to describe him. "He was a figure, I would dare say, who was indefinable. One could attribute to him all possible adjectives: he was paternal, he was austere; he was frowning, he was cheerful; he was sarcastic, he was ironic. His eyes scrutinized a person as if he were piercing into their flesh, and forced you to look down."

After he entered the sacristy, Padre Pio cordially greeted and spoke with a certain gentleman who was standing near Alfredo. This man, as soon he saw the priest approach, went down on his knees and proceeded to kiss the friar's hand. Then Padre Pio, as part of his preparation for leading the Vespers ceremony, made use of a little water basin that was nearby, and washed his fingers which extended from the half-gloves of wool he wore over his stigmatized hands. As he finished, that same gentleman hastily retrieved a white handkerchief from his pocket and gave it to Padre Pio so he could dry his hands. Padre Pio returned it to him, and he put it back in his pocket. But as the priest was exiting the sacristy to enter the church, the gentleman again took out the handkerchief, carefully folded it, and placed it in his attaché case.

Alfredo was watching all this happen, and the man, seeing his curiosity, told him that he would explain everything when Vespers was over. They introduced themselves, and went into the church for the ceremony. Afterwards, they went out into the piazza in front of the church, and the mysterious gentleman said to Alfredo, "Now, I will satisfy your curiosity about the handkerchief, by telling you my story."

It turns out that the man was a medical doctor, whose name Alfredo can not recall. He had been coming to San Giovanni every week for the past six months. He intended to keep returning until Padre Pio's hospital was finished, and then he would remain at San Giovanni to dedicate his life to the sick and suffering. His home was at Rome, where he practiced his medical profession. He was a confirmed atheist, as was his late father before him, who also had been a doctor. But his father, although an unbeliever, was a person of great humanity. "The first thing that he taught me as soon as I had reached the age of reason, was that I must always and unconditionally help and assist those who suffered in any way, materially or morally."

He was single, and lived in the same apartment complex where his older sister lived with her husband and son. His sister and brother-in-law were both practicing Catholics, but he admired their discretion in never trying to involve him in a discussion of religion. In point of fact, he did not even know what the inside of a church looked like! Their 21 year old son, Massimo, was a third year medical student, following in the footsteps of the family tradition.

About eight months ago Massimo began complaining about severe headaches. As a doctor, the gentleman attributed his nephew's headaches to exhaustion due to his intensive studies in order to excel in his tests and exams. He prescribed analgesic painkillers for him, but the headaches continued. Then he had Massimo undergo a series of blood tests, which proved to be normal, except for anemia, which was attributed to the fact that his appetite was poor, causing him to eat little. Since there was still no improvement in his condition, recourse was had to an electroencephalogram. The EEG revealed, to the terror of the family, that Massimo was suffering from a brain tumor!

It was hard for them to accept this frightening conclusion, and he personally took his nephew to a famous clinic in Switzerland, which unfortunately confirmed the diagnosis. Not convinced, his uncle took him to an illustrious medical doctor based in London, who subjected Massimo to a barrage of tests and radiographs. After careful analysis of the results, this doctor determined that Massimo only had three or four months to live. What was worse, there was no hope for a surgical intervention, since the location of the tumor in his brain was such that an operation to remove it would result in total paralysis of the patient, or even death.

When he returned to Rome from England with Massimo, the gentleman told his brother-in-law the full truth of the situation; but to his sister, Massimo's mother, he told the "pitiful lie" that with time and the proper treatment, her son would improve. The London doctor had prescribed extra-strong painkillers, since with the passage of time the sufferings would become atrocious. With these analgesics, it almost seemed as if Massimo were improving for a time, but the destructive force of the cancer was inexorable. He was forced to abandon all of his studies, and then his general physical wasting and malnutrition confined him to bed. The tumor attacked his optic nerves, and little by little he became blind.

Massimo's mother was altogether desperate, and turned her prayers to all the saints of Paradise! His uncle visited the bedside daily, trying to inspire hope and courage in the young man. Then he was constrained to leave his patient behind for a few days in order to attend an important medical conference in Milan. While he was gone, Massimo began to experience shooting pains that were so bad that he could not stand them, and his mother was forced to have recourse to another doctor, who was highly qualified, and also very religious. This new doctor, after seeing Massimo and the results of the x-rays and tests, realized the situation had become grave. He told his mother that the medicines prescribed by the London physician were the best available, but that in Massimo's situation, science was impotent. "A miracle was the only hope, and they still happen even today, although most people are unaware of it." She must pray, continued the doctor, because Massimo has need of prayers more than of medicine. Massimo's mother had a special devotion to St. Gemma Galgani, and taking a little statue of the saint, she placed it under the pillow of her son, who had now become a mere specter.

When the uncle returned from the conference in Milan the next morning, he was rather upset that another doctor had been called in to see Massimo, but he refrained from saying anything to his sister.

However, when he discovered the figurine of St. Gemma under the pillow of his patient, the confirmed atheist behaved like a beast and raged against his sister for believing in such things, and left the house infuriated.

When he returned to see his patient that afternoon, he witnessed what he considered to be an incident of alarming fanaticism. At his sister's home a group of about ten family members and friends, people that he personally respected, even though they were all fervent Catholics, had made a circle in the bedroom of Massimo. They had placed him him the center of the group, having him kneel on a cushion and leaning him on a chair for support, while they all recited the Rosary for his healing. Among them, perhaps the most fanatical but also the man the doctor most revered, was an elderly, retired ex-colonel, who was a spiritual child of Padre Pio.

At the sight of this dreadful gathering, the doctor left the room, complaining loudly about his sister and brother-in-law. Because of their religious fantasies, they could not even allow their son Massimo the joy of dying in peace in his bed! He continued to vilify the group, who could hear his imprecations, but they continued to faithfully pray the Rosary. At its conclusion, the retired military man said to them, "Now let us offer a particular prayer to Padre Pio, asking him to intercede with the Lord and to assist me in what I am about to do. I have a handkerchief that the saintly friar had used some time ago to wipe his stigmatized hands. With this cloth, I will cover the head of Massimo, and God will do the rest."

Upon hearing these words, the doctor stormed back into the room like a madman. Seeing the ex-colonel place the handkerchief upon Massimo's head, the doctor turned towards the retired soldier, angrily shouting that although he had the utmost respect for him, he would like give both him and his Padre Pio a good kick!

He had barely finished pronouncing this threat when Massimo suddenly yelled out, "Mama, Papa, I can see you!" Staggering, he tried to get to his feet. His uncle grasped him under the armpits so that he would not fall, and placed him on his bed. Then the bewildered doctor, feeling pale and drained like an old rag, and stripped of his anger, cast himself down on a chair. Minutes later, Massimo, who was being fed intravenously, asked his mother for something to eat. Crying tears of joy, she hurried to prepare him a bit of pastina, which he eagerly consumed, without bringing it back up as usually occurred.

As the days passed, Massimo grew better before their very eyes. After about three weeks, he was given all the x-rays and tests as before, but this time the result was different. The tumor in his brain had completely disappeared! Another disappearance was the atheism of his uncle, the doctor. "My transition to Christianity was so rapid that I did not even notice it. It seemed to me that I had always been Catholic."

Soon after, he was awakened one evening by someone calling out his name. Startled, he thought it was the voice of Massimo's father. Now wide awake, he again heard that same voice. But this time it said, "Don't forget that I am waiting for you, because you promised to give me a good kick!" Immediately aware of who it was, he got dressed and packed a suitcase, even though it was only 2:00 am. Taking a taxi, he was rushed to the Termini station in Rome, where he boarded the 3:30 am train for Foggia. He arrived at San Giovanni Rotondo around noon and went to the friary church of St. Mary of the Graces.

In the afternoon, Padre Pio came down from his cell to hear the confessions of the men. As he walked past Massimo's uncle, even though he had never seen him before, Padre Pio grabbed the doctor by the arm and took him to confession. The man went down on his knees, and Padre Pio said to him, "Here I am, I am all yours!" He cried for a long time, as Padre Pio talked to him: "Do not torment yourself because you have time ahead of you to make amends. Be calm because you are neither the worst nor the last. You were confounded because you were not meant to be as you were. Now that you are here I can tell you some beautiful news:

your father, who was an atheist as you were, is saved and is with your mother. So now you can see that the mercy of God is great, and he abandons no one."

Padre Pio continued, "At this place we are in the process of constructing a hospital for the relief of the suffering of so many poor people, and since you are a medical doctor, I would like you to come to work in this hospital." The doctor replied, "Padre, there is nothing in the world that will make me leave this place. I will stay here until and I die, and you can do with me as you will."

And that is the story that the gentleman with the handkerchief related to Alfredo.

"And God wrought by the hand of Paul more than common miracles. So that even there were brought from his body to the sick, handkerchiefs and aprons, and the diseases departed from them, and the wicked spirits went out of them." [Acts 19: 11, 12.]

Based on a two-part article by Alfredo Lapertina in the "Voce di Padre Pio" magazine issued by the friary in San Giovanni Rotondo, February 1995 (pp. 23-25) and March 1995 (pp. 27-29).

XII. PADRE PIO'S MASTERPIECE

Giacomo Gaglione, the spiritual child of Padre Pio that most resembled him.

Giacomo Gaglione first met Padre Pio not long after the friar had received the gift of the stigmata in the choir loft of the little church of St. Mary of the Graces, at San Giovanni Rotondo. He had read about him in 1919 in one of very first newspaper articles about Padre Pio, that related the wonders of this new miracle worker from an obscure town in the poverty-stricken south of Italy. The article caught the attention of Giacomo because it spoke glowingly of prodigies and cures reportedly as a result of the prayers of this monk, and Giacomo desperately needed a cure. For the past seven years he had been almost completely paralyzed by a rare form of polyarthritis. He was in constant pain, and could only find some relief by lying in a specially constructed iron wheelchair that had to be set at a 45 degree angle. He was not able to speak, but since his fingers and hands could move, he was capable of writing.

He contracted this illness suddenly and unexpectedly when he was a young teenager about to finish his secondary education. He came from a prominent family with a long line of lawyers on his father's side, going back to the 1600's, and his mother was from the wealthy nobility. Born in 1896 in Marcianise, in south-central Italy, he was the first of many children, and had all the advantages, materially and socially, that would presage a brilliant career. He had been extremely active in sports, especially cycling which was gaining popularity at that time, even entering and winning some races. Athletic, intelligent and handsome, it is not surprising that he was especially popular with the young ladies.

All this changed practically overnight when he was only sixteen years old. It began with a sharp pain in the heel of his right foot, and in a few days his feet and legs began to swell. The pain was atrocious, and soon he was unable to move any of his limbs. In a very short time, he became an invalid who had to be spoon-fed by his mother. His affluent family used every possible means to determine what was wrong and how to cure him, but medical science was at a loss. The very best specialists were consulted, and everything from massages to visits to a geothermal spring were tried. Even surgery proved useless.

However, Giacomo continued to believe that some day he would be healed, and he actually made plans to marry a girl who lived in an apartment in the same palazzo. This dream fueled his hope and gave him a reason for living. Apparently they were in love, and their friendship was accepted by both families for a time. But eventually the girl's mother realized that she did not want her daughter to spend her life caring for an invalid, no matter how illustrious or wealthy his family was. She persuaded Giacomo's mother to put an end to the relationship. But his mother knew that this would be a great blow to Giacomo, and she could not deliver it herself. Instead she asked the family priest to gently break the news to her son. As the priest approached the subject with him in a round-about way, Giacomo quickly understood what he meant, and that his hopes were destroyed. Screaming, he tried to grab a scissor that was nearby, in a vain attempt to end his life. From then on he had to be watched constantly. He became rebellious, rancorous, blasphemous, and had lost the will to live.

It was in this state of mind and soul that he first heard of Padre Pio. The article he saw in the paper was not just a short notice, but rather an extensive report made by journalist Renato Trevisani, who had been specifically assigned by his employer, a major Neapolitan newspaper, to throughly investigate and report on the phenomena associated with the mysterious Franciscan friar. Initially skeptical, the writer became sold on the saint after spending a week at San Giovanni.

He wrote without reserve about how the blood of the stigmata allowed Padre Pio to intercede before God to perform miracles, and Trevisani spoke directly with people who had been healed.

As Giacomo read through this article, which consumed six columns of the newspaper, hope began to return to him. He announced to the family his intention to go and see Padre Pio, and was quite enthusiastic about making the journey. He became convinced that he would return from San Giovanni Rotondo completely cured. He even began to re-kindle his relationship with the girl he wanted to marry some day. But all this frightened his family, who were concerned that if a cure were not obtained, it would certainly be devastating – the end of everything for Giacomo. Consequently, they did their best to dissuade him from making such a fatiguing trip. Giacomo would not hear of it and wanted to go whatever the difficulties.

Finally, a group pilgrimage was organized, comprised of his parents, some aunts and uncles, various friends, and the family doctor. The trip was grueling. First, they spent six hours in a crowded train compartment. Next they had to wait five hours in Bari in search of a vehicle capable of transporting Giacomo and his customized wheelchair. Then he was forced to spend the next five hours stretched out on a car seat with his head protruding out a window, during a raging storm, before reaching San Giovanni Rotondo.

Finally Giacomo found himself before Padre Pio. He had been waiting for this encounter for months, in order to ask for a cure of the painful malady that had immobilized him for the past seven years. First he made his confession. But then, as he later wrote: "Padre Pio looked at me with his eyes so deep and so beautiful and smiled at me, with the smile of an innocent child. To see Padre Pio and to forget the reason for my journey were one and the same event." He had found a treasure greater than the cure he had sought. He understood that his destiny was not to be cured, but to accept his sufferings as Padre Pio did; as a sharing and collaboration in the redemptive sufferings of Christ for the salvation of others. The veil that hides the mystery of the value of suffering was lifted; he saw that enduring the immobilization of his entire body on his cross of iron was similar to Padre Pio's carrying the wounds of Christ on his hands, feet and chest. Giacomo was healed when he ceased to desire a healing.

He now comprehended the true value of his own life, and knew that this call to carry his own cross was the will of God. This calling, that was communicated to him while gazing at the expressive eyes and smile of Padre Pio, was strong and clear. He stated later, "During this encounter with Padre Pio he performed a surgical operation; he removed my head and gave me another one in its place. [Mi ha tolto una testa e me ne ha messa un'altra.] If it is a miracle to make a paralyzed young man walk again, it is even more of a miracle to make him welcome with joy, for his entire life, the will of God." Padre Pio could have asked the Lord for his healing, but instead he saw that this man had the makings of a hero, with a strong soul, daring heart, and tenacious will, that could brave this Calvary.

When he returned home he began a new existence. His family and friends realized that he had become a different person. Now he was cheerful and happy, he laughed and joked, his visage reflecting an inner joy. From then on, Giacomo was a man "crucified with a smile." He would dedicate his entire life to caring for the sick and infirm, teaching them the immense value of suffering.

Giacomo was the spiritual child of Padre Pio that was the most similar to him. Just as Padre Pio bore the stigmata for fifty years, so did Giacomo remain crucified on his cross of iron for fifty years. Just as Padre Pio founded his hospital, The House for the Relief of Suffering, so did Giacomo found the movement of The Apostolate of Suffering. He represented one of the most electrifying miracles wrought by God through the intercession of the Padre. The two men continued to remain in touch with each other, and the "perfume" of Padre Pio often filled his house, as he appeared to Giacomo in bilocation.

Many people sought him out for advice and

counsel. He could move his hands, and with these he wrote some 3,500 letters a year to the infirm who sought a word of consolation. He founded a periodical, published articles and books, and organized pilgrimages to Lourdes, Loreto, and of course San Giovanni Rotondo. In one book he wrote: "The sick person is the most sensitive person on earth: one smile can exalt him or a certain look can plunge him into a deep and fearsome moral isolation. The infirm person has the mission to glorify the Lord and help sustain creatures in His grace."

In May of 1962 he approached his final Calvary, his body covered with painful blisters. Visited by one of the friars, Giacomo asked him to write Padre Pio to obtain the grace that he could die in the month dedicated to Mary. Padre Pio assured him that the grace was obtained. When he passed away on May 28, 1962, his funeral in Marcianise was a triumph; the police barely managed to hold back the crowds. Padre Pio sent a telegram to his family: "With Jesus on the cross, with Jesus in holy Paradise." When asked if he was a saint, Padre replied, "A saint? Giacomo is a great saint!"

His cause for canonization has been initiated, and in April 2009 Pope Benedict XVI declared him to be Venerable Giacomo Gaglione, in recognition of his heroic virtues.

The information for this article came primarily from Renzo Allegri's *Padre Pio, Il Santo dei Miracoli*, pp. 137-142; also from an article by Stefano Campanella in *Voce di Padre Pio* magazine, December 2007, and from other sources.

XIII. SHE WAS CURED TWICE BY PADRE PIO

Maria Pennisi of Pietrelcina was attending the college of the Ursulines in Benevento. It was 1922, and from the start of that school year she had not been feeling well. She was tormented by constant coughing and difficulty in breathing, and had no appetite. She was also suffering from intense pains in her right shoulder. When her parents came to the school to visit her and realized the condition she was in, they pulled her out of the college and sent her to live with her aunt in the hills of Avellino, hoping that breathing the fresh mountain air would help her.

But this change of venue failed to restore her health. Consequently her father, Carmine, took Maria to Naples to be examined by one of the more renowned physicians of that time, Dr. Castronuovo. He diagnosed that Maria was in the advanced stages of tuberculosis, with little hope of a recovery. She might die before the end of the year. Terrorized by this appalling news, Carmine took Maria to see the esteemed Dr. Giuseppe Moscati, now a canonized saint of the Church. Moscati confirmed the prior diagnosis, stating that the medical knowledge of the time could do nothing to save her.

Carmine and Maria returned to Pietrelcina, and in the weeks that followed, her condition continued to worsen. In his desperation, Carmine began to think of Padre Pio. Although now a monk in San Giovanni Rotondo, he had been born in Pietrelcina. "He is our countryman," Carmine thought to himself. "He has cured so many people, why should he not be able to cure my daughter?" Thus, along with some family members, Carmine and Maria traveled to San Giovanni to ask Padre Pio for the grace of a healing.

Although from Pietrelcina, Padre Pio did not know Maria and had never met her father, since Carmine had emigrated to America during much of the time the Padre was residing in that city. Yet, even though he had not seen her before, when Padre Pio first encountered her he said: "You are Maria Pennisi. You are feeling sick? You are mistaken, you are are healthier than I am. Your lungs are of steel!" Carmine, when he heard this, objected. "Padre, my daughter is very ill. The doctors say her case is hopeless. You are a saint, you alone can save her!" Padre Pio became more serious. He looked at Maria and then told Carmine, "Don't worry about this, I will take care of it."

The very next day Maria began to feel better. She wanted to go up the hill to the monastery on foot.

Carmine accompanied her, and marveled in seeing that she did not tire from the climb. Every morning thereafter, Maria arose early and walked to the church to attend Padre Pio's Mass. In about a week's time, her coughing had almost come to a halt, she was no longer bringing up any blood, and the pain in her right shoulder was completely gone.

Her dad Carmine was overjoyed. He decided that they could return home to Pietrelcina. He had some outstanding business affairs that required his attention, and he wanted Maria to resume her studies with the Ursulines. He went to the friary to thank Padre Pio, and to inform him that they were leaving. But the Padre replied, "Your daughter should not go back to school until after the holidays. If you must return to Pietrelcina, do so, but Maria needs to stay here a little longer." Carmine objected: "But Padre, you are a saint, you can protect Maria even from afar." Padre Pio answered, "No, your daughter will be fine if she remains here. Remember that the eye of the master fattens the horse." [Italian proverb meaning that a business thrives when the owner himself – in this case Padre Pio - personally oversees it.]

Carmine Pennisi paid no attention to the advice of Padre Pio. He returned to Pietrelcina with Maria, and had her resume her studies. But after only a few days back at school, she fell ill again. This time the doctors diagnosed it as a case of pleurisy. When Padre Pio was later informed, he said, "I told them. If she had stayed in San Giovanni she would not have fallen sick." Her case became very serious, with a fever of 104, and she began to grow weaker with each passing day.

Then one evening in early January of 1923, Maria received a visitor. It was a woman who had just returned from San Giovanni Rotondo. She was a spiritual child of of Padre Pio, and brought several items associated with him to keep as relics. She offered to rub the chest of Maria with a piece of cloth that was stained with blood from the Padre's stigmata. Maria's parents gave their consent. Almost as soon as the relic touched her, she began to feel better, and then she dozed off for about an hour. When she awoke her temperature was taken – it was now 98.6 degrees! Maria confidently concluded, "It was Padre Pio."

The next day Doctor Andrea Cardone came to check on Maria, and when he saw that the temperature was completely normal, he was convinced that the thermometer was broken. He used another one, and it too read 98.6 degrees. "Impossible!" said Cardone, who had been Padre Pio's doctor in Pietrelcina for many years. He then subjected Maria to a meticulous battery of respiratory tests, but could find nothing amiss. There was no longer any trace of the pleurisy; Maria was completely cured.

Her father Carmine went to see Padre Pio to tell

him the good news, and to ask if Maria could now return to school. "You must wait another twelve days," said the Padre. And this time, Carmine knew enough to follow Padre Pio's advice. Maria did return to school after that short wait, and was able to finish out the school year. All told, she had missed 53 school days because of her two illnesses, and yet she finished first in her class! When she returned to San Giovanni to personally thank Padre Pio, he replied, "Give thanks to the Lord, who has stopped your coughing and cured you again this time. You must give thanks to Him and to no one else."

Postscript: Letters exist which Padre Pio personally wrote to Carmine Pennisi and to Maria. There is one to Carmine and there are three to Maria. They date from May 1922 to February 1923, just prior to the time Padre Pio was ordered by the Holy Office in Rome to no longer write any letters. The letter to Maria dated February 7, 1923 was written to her while she was recovering from her attack of pleurisy. It reads, in my own unofficial translation:

"Dearest Marietta, May Jesus and Mary watch over you with benevolent eyes to render you always dearer to their hearts! I am very sorry to hear about your illness, but I thank Jesus who has quickly dealt with the malady. Strive to rest for a few more days before resuming your studies. I never cease to recommend you always to Jesus, together with all of your family. Be of good spirits and don't worry about anything. Study and always be a lover of Christian piety, living tranquilly. Best wishes to your parents, and if you happen to see any of my family [in Pietrelcina] say hello to them for me."

Ironically, Maria herself became part of Padre Pio's extended family, by marrying into the DeNunzio's, the family of Padre Pio's mother. Her recently deceased daughter, Graziella DeNunzio Mandato, wrote a book about Padre Pio, and her grandson Fr. Pio Mandato is a priest living in the USA.

This story is based primarily on the account in Renzo Allegri's *Padre Pio Il Santo Dei Miracoli*, pp. 164-167; additional information from *Padre Pio Storia D'una Vittima*, Vol. 1, pp. 288-290, by Francobaldo Chiocci and Luciano Cirri.

XIV. PADRE PIO AND THE ANGELS

Mr. P. Biavati was on his way to San Giovanni Rotondo to attend Padre Pio's Mass and make his confession to him. He began his journey in the morning, leaving from Florence, quite a distance away from saint's friary. But the traffic was very heavy on the main highway heading south, the "Autostrada del sole," which incidentally is the oldest European motorway. The congestion on the road caused him serious delays, and instead of reaching San Giovanni by sundown, he had only gone as far as Naples. Tired and agitated from the drive, he thought it would be best to stay overnight there, and then proceed the next morning. Before exiting the Autostrada, he stopped at a rest stop for some coffee, three cups in fact. This made him feel so refreshed and awake that he scrapped his plans to stay in Naples that night, and instead decided to drive the rest of the evening to his destination, a distance of about 135 miles.

It was late at night by the time he left the Autostrada and took the road to San Giovanni Rotondo.

The drive would take almost three hours, but amazingly Mr. Biavati remembers nothing at all of the trip! All he can recall is starting the engine, and putting his hands on the steering wheel. The next thing he can remember was his car approaching the square in front of Padre Pio's friary. At that point, someone shook him on the shoulder, and said, "Come on, now, take over!" Fearful and confused, he parked the car, rested awhile, and then made his way to the church for Padre Pio's early morning Mass. After the Mass ended, he was able to approach Padre Pio to tell him how astonished he was to ride all the way from Naples, without remembering that he drove the car at all. But Padre Pio replied with a smile, "You are right. You were sleeping all the way and my guardian angel was driving for you!"

Kevin Hale, who lives in the Chicago area, visited San Giovanni Rotondo for a week in January of 1965 where he attended the 5:00 am Mass at the friary church. When Padre Pio took off his half-gloves during the Mass, Kevin was able to clearly see, from his vantage point, the marks of the stigmata on the saint's hands. One morning he took a crucifix with him to Mass, which he had purchased at a nearby religious goods store. Afterwards in the sacristy, Padre Pio came to bless each person there. Kevin extended his hand with the crucifix as Padre Pio approached him. Seeing the crucifix, he blessed it, kissed it, and then pressed it to Kevin's lips for him to kiss it also. Then Kevin kissed

Padre Pio's hand, and when he did so he immediately smelled a strong, sweet fragrance, similar to cinnamon and roses. The aroma stayed with Kevin for almost an hour.

One night at his hotel before going to sleep, Kevin prayed to his guardian angel. He asked him to go to visit Padre Pio and tell him about all of his spiritual needs. The following evening, he joined the villagers and pilgrims outside in the square by Padre Pio's monastery cell, to bid him goodnight. He came to the window and gave everyone his blessing, speaking something in Italian to the group. Kevin asked a woman standing next to him, who spoke English and Italian, to tell him what Padre Pio had said. She told Kevin that Padre Pio said that he had been kept awake the previous night by an American's guardian angel!

Two young girls, who were neighbors, lived with their families in San Giovanni Rotondo. One night, they stayed over together in one of their houses. They did a lot of talking before going to bed, and the conversation got around to a famous person living right in their own town, Padre Pio. They were at the age when religion was beginning to make an impression on them, and they had heard that Padre Pio has a special relationship with the angels. They were discussing the report that anyone could send their own guardian angel to him to deliver special messages.

They realized that this was not an opportunity to miss. So one of the girls said, "I am going to send my guardian angel to Padre Pio to ask him to cure my uncle Fred." The other girl declared that she would send her angel to ask for a cure for her cousin. And so it went during the evening, until the two girls fell asleep. The next morning after Mass, the girls went to receive Padre Pio's blessing in the sacristy (this was in the early days, when women were allowed in the sacristy of the friary). But to their surprise, Padre Pio seemed angry at them. He said that their guardian angels had kept him up all night long. First one asked for prayers for her Uncle Fred, then another arrived with a request for prayers for her cousin. "And you kept it up all night long," he said. "I didn't get any sleep!"

But he was not really angry, he was just trying to point out to them that their angels did really do what they were told. We know this because of what he said to one of his spiritual daughters, Carmela Marocchino, who lived near the friary at the home of Mary Pyle. Carmela wanted to send her angel to him very late one night, but did not do so because she was worried about disturbing Padre Pio's rest. When she told him this, he replied, "You may send your guardian angel any time of day or night, as I am always happy to receive him."

A husband and wife were making a weekend trip to their vacation villa by the sea on the coast of Italy. They were leaving from Rome on a Saturday evening, and planing to spend a few days there to ready the place for the summer months. Traveling with them was their fairly large French poodle. About a dozen miles before turning off from the main highway, the Via Aurelia, to reach their destination, their auto broke down. They pushed it to the shoulder of the busy thoroughfare, hoping that someone would stop and give them assistance. But car after car just sped by, and no one bothered to stop and help them.

They had patiently waited by the roadside for about two hours, and it was starting to get dark. Finally the wife told her husband that they should pray to Padre Pio so that he would send an angel to help them out in this predicament. Padre Pio was still alive at the time, and she had previously spoken to him about guardian angels. Her husband was not too enthusiastic about this suggestion, but he told her to go ahead and try.

Not more than ten minutes later a black car approached, slowed down and stopped at the disabled vehicle of the beleaguered couple. Out stepped a very handsome young man, of aristocratic countenance, and well-dressed in blue. He asked them what had happened. After the husband explained their situation, the stranger confidently announced that he would take care of the problem and fix everything. He lifted the hood of the car to inspect the engine, although the husband, who was an experienced driver, had already done this without finding the problem. But the young man said to him that the radiator had lost all its water and was burnt out. He told him to take the empty can and fill it with water. There was a nearby farmhouse with a well from which he could draw the water.

The husband reached into the trunk for an empty can, and automatically headed for the farm house which was on the other side of the busy highway. Although normally it was extremely hazardous to cross the Via Aurelia on foot, he reached the other side with ease. While he was gone, the stranger in blue fetched a black box from his own car. Taking out a roll of adhesive tape, he proceeded to seal up the radiator. The wife, who was silently watching everything, was amazed at seeing his elegant and tapered hands, gracefully performing the task at hand. She also noticed that her dog, the French poodle, was also watching the man quietly and calmly, although he normally would bark at strangers.

After the husband safely re-crossed the Via Aurelia to return with the can of water, the young man filled the radiator and closed the hood. He told the couple that they could continue on safely, especially since they were quite near their destination. But tomorrow they should not fail to take their car to be checked out. They thanked the man profusely, and with a smile he said goodbye to them, and got into his car which was right in front of theirs. Since it was now nightfall, the couple entered their car and quickly turned the headlights on. The wife was eager to read the license plate of the stranger's car before it pulled away. But there was no license plate! Instead, there was a long white strip filled with what appeared to be hieroglyphics. She could see everything clearly since the cars were still going slowly, and there were no standard numbers or letters where the license plate should be, to indicate a place of origin. They proceeded onward until the couple approached their turn-off from the highway. They occupants waved good-bye to each other from their cars. The pair expected to see the stranger just continue along on the Via Aurelia, but suddenly they could no longer see his car – it had disappeared!

They reached their vacation villa in a rather dreamy state, pondering over what had just occurred. The stranger came directly to them, he knew that there was an empty can in their car, and knew they were close to their home, although they never mentioned their destination to him. The failure of their dog, who was always wary of strangers, to bark at him was perplexing. They could not fathom why there was no license plate on his car, just a strip of hieroglyphics. Finally, whenever they drove on that section of the Via Aurelia in the future, they never could find that farmhouse with the well.

The wife later said that Padre Pio confirmed to her that it was an angel who had come to their aid. The saint had heard her prayer to send them a heavenly helper, and Padre Pio does not disappoint! This story is drawn from a report by Padre Alessio Parente (see below), who lived with Padre Pio for years. Padre Alessio affirms that the adventure, although incredible and unusual, is true.

This chapter is primarily based on accounts found throughout the book *Send Me Your Guardian Angel*, by Padre Alessio Parente. The Kevin Hale story is based on an interview in *Pray, Hope and Don't Worry* by Diane Allen, pp. 275-6.

XV. PADRE PIO AND THE ANGLICAN MINISTER

As the Reverend Eric Fisher laid his healing hands upon the infirm leg of Alice Jones, she was astonished to see his face transform into the face of Padre Pio

The Reverend Eric Fisher is an active Anglican priest of the Church of England, who has dedicated his life and ministry to the healing of suffering souls and bodies. He wrote of his experiences in his best-seller from 1993, *Healing Miracles*. It was in the early 1970's, not long after being advised by his bishop that his role in the Church would be the healing ministry rather than parish work, that he first came to hear about Padre Pio. While he was at the home of experienced Anglican healer, Mary Rogers, in order to seek her advice, an Italian lady arrived. She often called on Mary when she visited from Italy. Noting that she was quite uncomfortable in his presence, Fr. Fisher discretely left the room for a short time. Upon his return, the Italian woman told him that her being disturbed at his presence in the room was nothing personal – she had an aversion to all priests. That is, all but one. "There is only one that I like and that is Padre Pio."

After that incident, Fr. Fisher was moved to read and learn more about this Padre Pio. Since then, he has come to consider Padre Pio his "brother in the spirit," and has been aware of his assistance on many occasions during his healing sessions. Of course, Fr. Fisher understands that it is Jesus Christ that is the ultimate healer. He feels that while the healing of ailing bodies is good in itself, it is the healing of hearts and minds that is the truly important objective.

In 1980, he was part of a mission team that was sent out to Haydock, which is near Liverpool. They were each asked to visit certain people that were on the local vicar's sick list. Among those assigned to Fr. Fisher was a middle-aged school teacher named Alice Jones, who lived with her husband in a modest home near the center of town. On his first visit, he found her tearful and depressed, and in a bitter state of mind. Alice could no longer experience any sensation in her left leg. Her left foot was twisted to one side, and her spine was out of alignment. Seven years before, while lifting some tables for a school function, she tripped and fell, seriously injuring her hip. Her back hurt since that time, and she had undergone a major spinal fusion operation, whereby bone from her hip was grafted onto her spine. She could barely walk, only with great difficulty, with the aid of elbow crutches, and by means of a splint which lifted her left foot slightly off the ground. The pain was intense, and she controlled it by an excessive use of alcohol and drugs. Like some others who had undergone a fusion operation, she felt she was on her way to becoming an alcoholic. The State had assessed her as one hundred percent disabled.

Before this visit to Alice, Fr. Fisher said a special prayer to Padre Pio from a novena prayer card, asking for his protection and support. He had also distributed these cards after morning Mass. They featured a picture of the saint, and gave an account of his austere life of service. Although Padre Pio had already passed on, the Anglican priest frequently prayed for his assistance.

Upon seeing Alice that first time, he began with a prayer for her and all the sick of the parish. Then he laid his hands on her back, running them up and down along her spine. Since her accident, her back had always felt icy cold, but surprisingly she now felt a sudden warm glow, which flowed down her spine and all around her. Fr. Fisher continued with his laying on of hands for about fifteen minutes, but then stopped. At the time he did not know why he ceased, but later became certain that it was Padre Pio protecting him from putting too much pressure on the spine, which might have affected the spinal fusion. After leaving the Jones' residence, and during a church service that evening, he asked Padre Pio for a miracle.

Returning to Alice's home the next day, he found her in a better state of mind and not as bitter, but she did not show any marked optimism or expectation. Fr. Fisher started again on her spine, and then began to treat her infirm left leg. He was curious as to why she had no sensation in it, since it seemed her calf muscles had not deteriorated. Then she abruptly exclaimed that she could feel "pins and needles" in a part of her leg, which also felt hot. She gradually experienced these sensations throughout the whole limb, even down to her twisted left foot. Then the priest concentrated his healing efforts on her ankle and foot, until it gradually straightened out and could rest flat on the floor. These changes were not accompanied by intense pain, although the operated part of the spine was probably affected.

Finally it was time for her to try and walk. Father urged her to try, but she insisted that she could not walk. Finally, after a seeming eternity, she raised herself up. Sobbing with joy, she began to hobble across the room. There was a deep silence felt throughout the house, and in his book Fr. Fisher wrote that it was similar only to what he "experienced on the rare occasions when something tremendous was happening."

Later that same evening Alice Jones told Father something that, unknown to him, was occurring during the healing process. She said that when she looked down upon him, she saw superimposed upon his face, the visage of an older man with a beard. Thinking it was a hallucination, she tried opening and closing her eyes, but the strange old personage was still there. Then she saw the old man, dressed in a monk's habit, standing by her side. He seemed to take over. She could hear Fr. Fisher's voice, but she also heard the older man speaking in a foreign language. He blessed her twice with the sign of the Cross, while repeating "Gesu`, Maria; Gesu`, Maria." With a great feeling of love and warmth, he took her arm, telling her to get up and walk in the name of Jesus. When she heard the voice commanding her to walk, her old fears of falling returned. But the word "walk" reverberated around in her head, and as it did, she gained a sense of confidence and faith, and overcame her fear of failure. She was utterly amazed that she could walk across the room to the door, and return to her chair! By then the old man had disappeared from her view; her pain and discomfort were gone, and once again she saw the face of Fr. Fisher.

Everyone was in an emotional state, and her daughter Lesley was in tears. Lesley became aware of a strong smell of perfume. Her baby son had been having sleeping problems since birth, and she felt compelled to stand with him behind her mother's chair. She experienced the sensation of being wrapped in a warm, comforting blanket. After Alice promised to attend a healing session that evening in the church, Fr. Fisher left, in order to take in what had happened. Hearing the news that she could walk, her husband Frank returned home from work early. She ran down the drive to meet him and they hugged each other with joy in their hearts. That night they went as a family to give thanks in the church. The parishioners gasped in amazement when they saw that Alice was walking. But she still had no idea who the "old man" was. Back home, she became emotional and told Frank that she had seen Moses. She slept well that night, without having to take any tablets or sleeping pills, but her husband was worried that this was all a dream, and he kept a vigil by the bed.

Frank was concerned that her previous condition might return, which would be a sad disappointment. But instead he was about to witness a further miracle. Every morning Frank dutifully packed an ulcer that had left a gaping hole in her left heel. That night he had readied the bandages that would be needed for dressing the wound. He warned Alice that it might be painful now that sensation in her left leg had returned. The next morning he prepared to dress the wound as usual, but the ulcer was no longer there! At first Frank thought she had given him the wrong leg. But there was no sign of the ulcer, not even a mark. They found the dressing rolled up in the bed. Frank wept, saying that it was a miracle.

That evening Alice returned to the church again to receive Holy Communion in thanksgiving. She felt that she was seeing everything with new eyes. The words of the liturgy became real, and it seemed that she was truly participating at the Last Supper. As she left the service, Fr. Fisher handed her one of the Padre Pio novena prayer cards. She realized at once that Padre Pio was the old man at the healing. She was relieved to find that he was a real person and not imaginary. But she was shocked to learn that he had died in 1968. And so began her quest to find out "Who is Padre Pio?"

Frank M. Rega

XVI. THE MANGIAPRETI

After Padre Pio received the stigmata on September 20, 1918 at San Giovanni Rotondo, some who lived in that area remained incredulous, and became his "enemies." One such man by the name of Michele lived in Torremaggiore, a small municipality about 25 miles to the west of San Giovanni. A clamorous incident occurred around the year 1919 involving Michele and Padre Pio, which was reported at the time in newspapers from eyewitness accounts.

Michele was a confirmed atheist and socialist. He was known as a "mangiapreti," (literally – a priest-eater), who harbored bitter resentment and hatred towards Catholic priests. An inveterate blasphemer, he considered Padre Pio to be a notorious deceiver.

He was proprietor of a furnace operation for the baking of terracotta clay used in ceramics and pottery. At that time the kiln was fired with bean and barley straw. Near the oven, Michele had two interconnecting rooms where he kept the supply of straw piled up.

However, for six straight days a strong gale was blowing throughout the area, such that it prevented him from igniting his oven. Unable to work, he began to blaspheme to no end. Further, since every day a stream of pilgrims and visitors would pass by his workshop on their way to Padre Pio's friary at San Giovanni Rotondo, he cursed him in particular.

One evening, on June 24th, the feast of St. John the Baptist, Michele prayed, "Dear Padre Pio, I will believe in you if you can put an end to this windstorm that keeps me from lighting my oven and from working." At that moment, a man entered the courtyard of the place, dressed in the garb of a humble sharecropper. He greeted Michele, and asked him if he had an ember with which he could light his pipe. At that, the artisan went into a rage. He railed that he has been cursing and swearing for six days because has not been able to fire his furnace.

The visitor replied that he would light the kiln himself. Michele became even more furious because he thought the man was mocking him. Taking hold of a pitchfork he came towards the stranger. He shouted to him, "Are you poking fun at me? Are you like that 'x&@#!' Padre Pio that makes miracles for the simpletons?" But the visitor remained calm and serene, while replying "I am Padre Pio."

Immediately, a a large and fearful tongue of fire

several meters in length issued forth from the oven. A terrified Michele fell to the ground in a faint. Then he heard a voice calling him: "Don't be afraid. Learn to trust in the Lord and stop blaspheming Him!" As he came to, he saw a friar smiling down at him. He recognized Padre Pio, who took him in his arms to carry him away from the burning fire. Then the saint departed, disappearing through a wall around the property.

In the meantime, the fire which had so mysteriously started in the oven continued to rage. The flames, leaping high and wide, reached the two rooms adjacent to the furnace, where the piles of straw were stored – but incredibly the straw was not consumed. Soon, many people ran up, some coming from afar, after seeing the night sky illuminated by the blazing inferno. Michele's friends and neighbors tried to extinguish the flames, but without success. The remarkable fire continued to burn throughout the night, until about eleven in the morning.

Inside the furnace there were many terracotta vases and pots that had been readied to be baked. The usual baking time was about an hour at most, but the fire in that kiln had been going for about a dozen hours straight. Michele was certain that everything in the oven had been destroyed or pulverized. Instead, when he checked it, he saw that all the ceramics were done to perfection, none were burned or cracked, and there was no waste to throw away as usually happened. The people were amazed at this, and cried out that it was a miracle. The crowd extolled Padre Pio, since Michele told them that the monk had saved him from the flames. The straw from the storage rooms that the fire had mysteriously left unharmed, was gathered by them and taken home in bunches as souvenirs and relics. Similarly, they took away all the vases and pots that had been flawlessly baked by the miraculous fire.

Michele was so upset by the entire occurrence that when he returned home, he had to be confined to bed with a very high fever. After he got better, he journeyed to San Giovanni Rotondo to thank Padre Pio. He had now became a fervent defender of the Padre, and finally ceased his blasphemies.

Based on a selection from Renzo Allegri's *Padre Pio Il Santo dei Miracoli*, pp. 102-104.

XVII. THE CURE OF A DESPERATE ILLNESS

An insatiable thirst caused her to drink countless gallons of water day and night.

For seven long years, beginning when she was only a teenager in 1945, Lucia Bellodi suffered from a severe case of diabetes insipidus, complicated by an earlier attack of encephalitis. She was a farm girl from Modena, in northern Italy, and had been admitted over the years to several hospitals and a sanatorium. The doctors did all they could with the knowledge then available, but instead of improving she only worsened. Suffering from a pituitary imbalance, she was declared incurable, and was ultimately admitted to a nursing home in Modena. At the nursing facility, a "home for the aged," the sisters did all they could to provide her relief from her most unusual illness, characterized by an insatiable thirst. Her body was unable to maintain adequate control over its water content, and as a result she had to constantly consume large amounts of water to offset her frequent urination. We are talking about drinking gallons and gallons of water per day, causing her abdomen to swell out of proportion. Incredible as it may seem, one source mentions 105 quarts of water, and by her own testimony, it had increased in the days before her cure to over 170 quarts in 24 hours.

She was enabled to sustain this affliction by drinking constantly through a rubber hose attached to a large container holding many gallons of water. Even at night when sleeping, she had to suck water out of the hose. If she did not keep drinking, her tongue would swell and her mouth would start to bleed. The nursing sisters looked after her continually, and due to urination complications, they were forced to change her bed linens many times a day. In addition, there was another extremely serious concern – about every two weeks there would be a crisis consisting of extremely painful headaches and high fevers, to the point of delirium.

Lucia held Padre Pio in great esteem, after learning about him from her hospital caregivers and the nursing sisters. Although she prayed to him often, it was not for the grace of a cure. Instead she asked him to intercede with the Lord so that she would be able to resign herself to accepting her malady, or to be freed from it by her death.

The day of Corpus Christi in 1952, she manifested to the sisters that she had a desire to attend Mass for the feast day. They agreed to this, but when she returned from making her confession, she was unable to stand. She was rushed to her bed, since this appeared to be the onset of one of her crises. The fever and headache lasted all that morning until the early afternoon, as she drank more and more water. At a certain point during that morning, she saw a friar, who looked at her fixedly with dark eyes, as if reproving her, but he said nothing. During her delirium, the nursing sister heard her say "Padre Pio, I can go on no longer; please come to take me!" Seeing how much Lucia was suffering, this sister too prayed that God would liberate her from such a pitiful existence.

At about two in the afternoon, at the culmination of the crisis, her caregivers thought that this was the end for her, as they felt her body getting cold. Lucia could smell all around her the sweet fragrance of the perfume of violets. As she wondered at this, she fell asleep. While she was sleeping, she heard these words: "Arise Lucia, since you are cured. This evening or tomorrow come to see me at San Giovanni Rotondo." As she slept, her mouth was firmly shut and the sisters could not insert the rubber hose so that she could continue to drink water. They were fearful that her tongue would swell and she would hemorrhage. Thus after an hour and a half of letting her rest, the sisters had to slap her into wakefulness. She awoke suddenly and got up from her bed, announcing to all that she was cured. At first they thought she was talking crazy, but after she explained what Padre Pio had said, they told her she should go into the chapel to thank the Lord.

She proceeded up the stairs on her own, feeling confident and secure, and even took part in the Corpus Christi procession. She felt completely well, as if she had never suffered at all for the past seven years. The doctors were summoned, and they could only conclude that a miracle had occurred. She expressed her wish to travel to Padre Pio's monastery in San Giovanni Rotondo, but they felt that she was not yet ready to sustain such a long trip, from the north of Italy to the south, and she was constrained to remain at the nursing home in Modena for three more days.

When she arrived at San Giovanni accompanied by two of the sisters, she was extremely happy to be able to see and to speak to Padre Pio, whom she thanked profusely. He smiled and said, "I was waiting for you," and he told her that it was the Lord who deserved the thanks. Upon her return to Modena, she moved in with her parents, and went to work on their farm. The doctors subjected her to a final battery of tests, which indicated that she was completely healthy. But they told her that because of her severe case of diabetes insipidus, she would never be able to have children of her own. However, confiding in Padre Pio, she chose to marry in 1961, and was blessed with a child.

This article is based on Lucia Bellodi's personal testimony, published in *Padre Pio Storia D'una Vittima*, by F. Chiocci and L. Cirri, pp. 670-672. Some additional information was provided by Rev. Bernard Ruffin in *Padre Pio the True Story*, pp. 336-337; and Rev. Charles Mortimer Carty, *Padre Pio the Stigmatist*, pp. 171-172. Where some of the details given in the latter two sources differ from the Chiocci-Cirri version, I have relied on Chiocci-Cirri since that source presented her own words.

Frank M. Rega

XVIII. THE ARTIST AND PADRE PIO

Antonio Ciccone is a world-renowned artist who has had hundreds of exhibitions and showings throughout Europe and the United States. One of the world's foremost portraitists, his works are to be found in museums and private collections from California to London. A spiritual child of Padre Pio, he grew up in San Giovanni Rotondo and was encouraged in his vocation by the saint. He is the artist responsible for two magnificent frescoes adorning the Church of Santa Maria delle Grazie in San Giovanni Rotondo. This is the church that was consecrated in 1959, and was at that time called the "new church" to distinguish it from the adjacent 16th century monastery chapel, where Padre Pio had received the stigmata. These two works are the *Resurrection* fresco and *St. Francis Receiving the Stigmata*. The room where they are located was once the Baptistery of the church, but now has been transformed into a place of prayer and devotion, enshrining the remains of Brother Daniele Natale, another spiritual child of Padre Pio.

After Antonio's First Holy Communion, which

he received from the stigmatized hands of Padre Pio, he began to sense his spiritual presence. He had great desire to be near him and started to frequent the friary, where he often made his confession to the saintly monk. Antonio says he owes everything to Padre Pio: career, family, children, success . . . and even his life.

One day he was at work high upon the scaffolding in order to paint one of these great frescoes in the church, working about fifty feet above the ground. In order to see from a distance the result of his labors, he started to descend on a ladder from the platform – but he made a misstep. Losing his balance, he found himself beginning to plunge below. Then all at once, an unexpected force pushed him and turned him around suddenly, so that he was able to grasp a rung of the ladder and hold himself firmly in place. Once he felt secure, he looked down below and saw Padre Pio, who was there and had seen everything. Immediately he understood that he was saved through the providential help of the Friar. "It is true, such help is always from God, but Padre Pio was his direct instrument."

At the year of his birth in 1939, His family had a farm not far from the friary. The first of nine children, his tasks included milking the cows and pasturing the sheep and goats. One day, while he was tending the animals, he raided a neighbor's cherry tree, unable to resist the temptation to taste them. The next time he saw Padre Pio in the confessional, before he could say anything, Padre Pio looked him straight in the eye and said, "And the cherries, they tasted good?" Anthony's face became redder than one of those cherries. He lowered his head and with a meek smile promised he would never do it again. Then Padre Pio gently touched his head, blessed him, and assigned him a very long penance. "I remember that I exited the confessional stunned but light-headed, my spirit was in the clouds."

As he grew older, he decided he did not want to be a farmer or rancher, but instead wished to be a painter. In fact, he had been drawing pictures from the age of 5. He loved to draw pictures of Padre Pio with a charcoal pencil, and admits that sometimes he went to confession just to observe and study up-close the particulars of his face. Sometimes the Padre would shoo him away from the confessional if it seemed Antonio was not there to make a sincere confession. But when he was 12 years old, he went to confession one day carrying a roll of drawings. Kneeling before the priest, Antonio told him that he wanted to study to be a painter, but his father could not afford it. "I am aware that you know so many people, Padre, throughout the world, and if you can help I will accept it willingly!" Then Padre Pio asked him what he was holding in his hands, and Antonio gladly showed him his drawings. One of them was of Padre Pio himself, but he was more interested in a drawing the budding artist had made of the Crucifixion by Guercino. "These are your own drawings?" he asked. After Antonio responded in the affirmative, the Padre said "E Bravo!" Then like a broken record, Antonio kept saying he wanted to be painter, and Padre Pio told him to have patience. "You will see that one day Divine Providence will assist you!"

In the evenings, Antonio along with others including Brother Daniele Natale and Padre Pellegrino, who were very close to Padre Pio, often accompanied him to the friary garden. There they sat down around the saint and listened with great attention as he recounted little stories and anecdotes. At the same time, Antonio would closely observe him to insure that his portraits and sketches would accurately resemble him. Often however, Padre Pio would seem annoyed at such intense scrutiny. "I did not look at him as the others did, but scrutinized him in order to impress his spirit in me. And he, in fact, every once in a while, stopped what he was talking about and looked right at me, saying, 'What are you looking at? Why are you looking at me that way?' I justified myself by admitting I was studying him, and he would respond with an engaging smile."

As time went on his skills and portfolio grew. With the support of Padre Pio, it was not long before Ciccone was able to find sponsors for his artistic endeavors, and he left home for Florence to study with the painter, Pietro Annigoni, famous for his portraits of Queen Elizabeth II. Periodically, about once a year,

Antonio returned to his family in San Giovanni Rotondo, and never failed to visit Padre Pio, who was eager to learn of his protégé's progress. "I told him about my experiences, and he would reply in his Benevento accent 'Don't make me lose face!' He reminded me to always thank God." Young Antonio, who was still rather timid and uneasy, liked to be accompanied on these visits by Padre Pio's friend, Brother Natale. Antonio would ask Padre Pio for a blessing for his friends, family and sponsors. "At these encounters, he would look at me intensely with his dark eyes, and with just a few words took away my anxieties, encouraging me to be confident and pray to the Lord, and to be patient with myself and others." He told the saint that certain situations were not easy to handle. The Padre responded, "It is for this very reason that you must pray and be patient! My child, if you cannot resolve on your own some problems, you must continue to humbly ask the help of our Heavenly Father, and patiently wait until you receive an answer."

But Padre Pio was not always easy on him. Sometimes he instilled in him a real fear. "I felt I was before a judge, a man strong in spirit, who with authority rebuked me for my indecisions, my thousands of excuses and delays, and forced me to meet, face to face, the responsibilities of life."

Antonio became settled in his career, and in addition to studying in Florence and working in parts of

Italy, he spent many years in the United States where his works were favorably received. He espoused an American woman, Linda, who bore him a daughter Tiana. With Padre Pio's blessing, the couple also adopted six children of various nationalities and ethnicities. Antonio currently maintains a spacious studio in the historical district of Florence.

When he was commissioned to paint the Resurrection fresco in the Baptistery of the Church of Santa Maria delle Grazie in San Giovanni, he approached Padre Pio to ask him for advice on how he could adequately represent such a magnificent event. But Padre Pio told him, "Do not be afraid, you will see that the right sentiments will unfold within yourself." Padre Pio passed by the fresco every morning to see its progress as Antonio worked on it. When it was completed, Padre Pio happily expressed his approval, joyful with the spirit of a child. "I realized how much the Padre, before art works or the so many things that happened to him, reacted like an innocent child. He was pleased just to look and appreciate, rather than analyze the techniques of how the painting was made."

While Antonio was working on the Resurrection fresco, he witnessed a dramatic event. A possessed woman began shouting and throwing herself down, striking her head on the marble floor, a prey to indescribable sufferings. Many people gathered around attempting to calm her, or at least keep her from hitting her head against the floor. Antonio had never seen anything like this, and was so petrified and shaken that he was unable to take any action. At a certain point, however, one of the bystanders, who had a prayer card with a picture of Padre Pio on it, laid it upon the woman. At the initial contact, she shrieked and cursed, slamming every part of her body on the floor. But shortly thereafter, she completely settled down, and an interior calm pervaded her. It was then that Antonio conceived the idea of painting such an event, and a year later he executed a compelling work showing a possessed woman being cured by Padre Pio: "The Healing." [See photo preceding the Table of Contents of this book.]

While he was in America working on a painting, he read about Padre Pio's death in the newspapers. "For me it was a day of great suffering and solitude. From that moment my thoughts of Padre Pio became more constant. Since I would no longer be able to visit him in person, I had to visit him within myself. At that period of time, I felt a special union with him. What struck me most was his humanity, the force and power of his attraction as a person. His soul was pure, totally rapt in God. I believe that Christ expressed Himself through him freely and openly, in childlike fashion. That is the explanation of the fascination that he exercised on the people that sought him out from all parts of the world."

Frank M. Rega

This article is based on a chapter from *I Miracoli che Hanno Fatto Santo Padre Pio*, by Enrico Malatesta, pp. 362-374.

XIX. HE BILOCATES TO THE POPE

By the mid 1920's there was a concerted effort by Padre Pio's enemies, including even his own bishop, to bring his ministry to a halt. False stories, rumors and accusations had reached the highest levels in the Vatican itself. As a consequence, in 1923 the Congregation of the Holy Office issued a public decree declaring that there was nothing supernatural in the ministry of Padre Pio, and therefore the faithful should act accordingly. In other words, the stigmata, miracles, cures, bilocation and conversions were not acknowledged by the Vatican. The Holy Office (now known as the Congregation for the Doctrine of the Faith), was responsible for the defense and promulgation of Catholic Doctrine.

Notwithstanding the decree, crowds continued to besiege the monastery, spurred on by the many who had been recipients of Padre Pio's charismatic gifts. Thus, in 1924 a new decree was issued, in which the Vatican repeated that nothing supernatural has been exhibited by Padre Pio, and the Holy Office again exhorted the faithful to abide by its decision. By 1925 many restrictions on his priesthood had been established, putting limitations on the length of his Mass, on his confessional, and his conversations with others. In addition, he could no longer correspond by letter with anyone, and was prohibited from seeing his long-time spiritual director.

This isolation of Padre Pio still did not satisfy his opponents, whose ultimate goal was to have him suspended entirely of his priestly ministry *a divinis* by Pope Pius XI. They swamped the Holy Office with calumnies and accusations, and its Secretary, Cardinal Merry Del Val, convinced the Pope that such a suspension was necessary. However, two high-ranking cardinals were avid supporters of Padre Pio: they were the Secretary of State Cardinal Gasparri, and Cardinal Sili, Prefect of the Tribunal of the Apostolic Signatura – the highest court of the Church. Hoping to achieve a consensus on the suspension, Pope Pius convoked a special, secret meeting to discuss the case of Padre Pio.

Present at the meeting with the Pope were the above-mentioned cardinals as well as five other cardinal "inquisitors" from the Holy Office. The discussion soon became heated due to the energetic defense of Padre Pio by his two supporters. However, the others remained firm in their opposition to him. The Pope appeared ready to decide in favor of the suspension *a divinis,* when suddenly there occurred "the most amazing charismatic episode that can be found in the lives of the saints."

The door to the meeting room opened, and a young Capuchin friar entered. The attendees were bewildered and shocked, since not only was he uninvited, but Swiss guards were supposedly protecting the entranceway. The monk had his hands hidden in the sleeves of his habit, and he seemed to walk with a slight limp. Before anyone could stop or interrogate him, he came directly towards the Pope. When he reached the Holy Father, he kneeled before him and kissed his feet. Then he pronounced these words: "Your Holiness, for the good of the Church do not permit this to occur." Kissing once again the feet of the Pontiff, he asked for his blessing, arose and left the room.

Just as soon as he departed, all the cardinals, recovering from their amazement, became very agitated. Some of them exited the room to demand from the guards why they had let this monk enter, in spite of the strict prohibitions against visitors. The surprised guards marveled at this, and said that they had not even seen any friar. The cardinals re-entered the room, and the Holy Father, having intuited what must have occurred, immediately suspended the meeting. He commanded them not to speak about the incident. However, with great solicitude he ordered Cardinal Sili to travel to San Giovanni Rotondo. The cardinal was to interrogate the Father Guardian of the Convent as to where Padre Pio was on that day and time, and what he was doing.

The sister-in-law of Cardinal Sili, the Countess Virginia Salviucci Sili, was a frequent visitor to San Giovanni, had confessed to Padre Pio, and had become one of his spiritual children. Aware of her devotion to the friar, the Cardinal invited her to accompany him on his mission, without telling her a word of what it was about. Upon their arrival at San Giovanni Rotondo, the Father Guardian told the cardinal that Padre Pio had not gone out of the friary that day, and at the time in question he was in the choir reciting the prayers of the daily Office.

Only at a later date did Cardinal Sili tell the Countess Sili the story about the bilocation of Padre Pio to the Pope. She in her turn related it to a priest who was her friend, confessor and a devotee of Padre Pio. His name was also Padre Pio – Padre Pio Dellepiane, of the order of Minims of St. Francis of Paola. The spiritual bond and mutual respect that existed between the two Pio's was such that the friar of San Giovanni Rotondo often recommended penitents to turn to Padre Dellepiane. St. Pio also said of him that although his name was Padre Pio Dellepiane, he was not Padre Pio of the Plains, but Padre Pio of the Peaks! Padre Dellepiane's own Cause for sainthood was opened in 1990, and on May 19, 2018 he was declared Venerable.

Venerable Padre Dellepiane carefully recorded the testimony of the Countess, writing that "I declare with an oath that the following is true." It is his handwritten report from 1966 that is the basis for the story of the bilocation of Padre Pio to Pope Pius XI. The outcome of the incident is that the suspension *a divinis* of Padre Pio from the priesthood never occurred. Although the Holy Office continued to persecute Padre Pio for years, the view of the Pope changed and Pius XI began to have a more favorable opinion of him.

This post is based on material from Chapters 9 and 10 of Renzo Allegri's *Padre Pio Il Santo dei Miracoli*. Additional information about Padre Dellepiane was obtained from the Internet.

Frank M. Rega

XX. JOURNEY INTO CREATION

Brother Daniele Natale was a Franciscan Capuchin, who passed away in 1994. He was one of Padre Pio's most devoted spiritual children and his close friend. For many years he was assigned to the friary at San Giovanni Rotondo, in the role of porter, questor, cook, and humble provider for the friars. In this way he grew in sanctity, and was the recipient of many spiritual favors from on High. After his death, his reputation for holiness was such that his body was moved to a special locus in the same church where Padre Pio himself had been initially interred, the Church of *Santa Maria delle Grazie*. His cause for canonization has begun.

In 1952 Fra Daniele, at the insistence of Padre Pio, underwent an operation for a tumor in his spleen at a hospital in Rome. For a certain period he submitted to radiation and chemotherapy at the clinic. It was during this difficult time in his life that he was granted a remarkable vision of God's creation. Daniele insists he was awake, sitting on his bed, and it was not a dream.

He found himself in an unknown place that he had never seen before – a beautiful countryside near a body of water. He began to walk along, and near a hedgerow he came upon an exceptionally gorgeous rose of a deep red color. It was marvelous to look at, and while admiring it he said, "How beautiful you are!" At the same time he could smell a perfume more heavenly than any fragrance he had ever experienced in his life. Full of amazement, he turned to the rose and said, "You are so beautiful, and with such a sweet aroma! How is it possible that you have not been discovered before?" The rose replied to Daniele, "I am from the Creator and am here in order to praise Him. As for the perfume, it serves to purify the air polluted by man, and to make up for the lack of love that man should show for his Creator." Hearing this Fra Daniele was troubled, since he thought that it was an accusation against him personally. "These words are for me," he thought. He felt a little relief when the rose replied, "No! They are not meant for you."

Resuming his walk in the countryside, he came before a garden bursting with flowers. He could not bring himself to tread upon them by continuing his walk. But the flowers, bending a little, invited him to proceed. Even as he apologized for trampling them, they in return thanked him. Turning towards the flowers, he asked, "Tell me, what is your task?" They answered, "To purify the air of sin and impurity, and to make up for the love which mankind lacks for the Creator." They were almost the same words of reproof spoken by the rose. And again he heard a voice saying that these words were not for him.

Continuing onward, he came to a little hill, at the bottom of which was a running brook which led to a pretty waterfall. Within himself he was thinking, "Is the water also going to tell me that it praises the Creator?" Then Daniele asked, "Sister water, what is your task before the Most High?" "To praise the Creator," was the reply. "And in what way do you praise the Creator?" he asked. "With my sounds," the water replied. Daniele then became aware that he had never heard rushing water sound such beautiful notes! From that little waterfall came forth the enchanting chimes of an organ, to which no man-made organ could compare. It was a truly celestial melody, that penetrated so deeply within the soul of Fra Daniele that he was forced to plead, "Enough! Enough!"

Then he began to walk along, stepping right in the brook itself, and yet he did not get wet. How curious! The brook led to the sea, and he found himself at a cove. The grass was beautiful and shiny, and the blades seemed to be statues pointing straight to the heavens. In their midst was an exquisite lily. It was tall, with a single flower in the form of a chalice – it was so attractive and enchanting to look at. But Daniele seemed to be in a hurry and did not linger there. However, he thought to himself that this lily too is going to tell me that it praises the Creator. So he continued walking, but the lily turned towards him as if to get his attention, and he said to it, "I already know, I know what your purpose is: to praise the Creator!" The flower then made a profound bow as if giving its assent, and he continued walking in the stream until he came to the sea.

He kept onward and walked right into the sea, not on the surface of the water but on the sea floor. It contained many beautiful plants, and a quantity of little fish that he had never seen before, thin and of various colors. They danced before him, and were so pretty, so attractive.

Then after going a few hundred feet, he noticed a very large fish coming towards him, confidently smiling at him. But Fra Daniele was afraid, and as it approached him, he told it to stop and tell him what it wants. But the great fish was mortified at having to keep away, and Daniele felt sorry for it. He exhorted the big fish to come closer. When it was only a few yards away, he asked the fish what his purpose was. "My task is to gather the praises of all creatures that live in the sea, and through the mediation of a priest who lives in the world, to offer them to the Creator." Daniele responded, "Oh I understand, that priest is Padre Pio." Upon hearing the name of Padre Pio, the large fish bowed profoundly, and remained that way until Fra Daniele asked him to straighten.

While walking on the sea bed, just as in the brook, he did not get wet. He marveled at it, and wondered to himself why. The waters themselves seemed to answer him, "You are here in our midst not merely as a man who has the weight of his body, but also as a spirit." That was why he did not get wet.

Returning to solid ground, he found himself on the banks of the sea, beyond the sand, where there were many bushes and rocks, and he came to a small hill. Looking around, he saw many little snakes of various pretty colors, similar to those of the little fish he had just seen. They twisted around each other, and as they swayed towards him, they seemed to be dancing in a marvelous way.

Then in the distance, on that little and pleasant hill, he saw a very large and long snake, that aroused fear in him as soon as he saw it. He kept turning away from it in order to avoid confronting it, but that snake somehow kept always in front of him.

Finally, Daniele was forced to ask it, "Perhaps you too wish to talk to me? Maybe you also are going to tell me that you snakes praise the Creator? But how can you praise the Creator if the devil has your appearance?" The great snake replied, "No, the devil does not look like us. It is mankind that has ascribed to the devil the appearance of a snake."

Then Daniele asked, "What is your praise, how do you praise the Creator?" "By our sounds." Immediately the serpents began to harmonize with each other and Daniele heard a sweet, penetrating melody. Once again, as with the enchanting sound made by the waterfall, he had to shout out, "Enough, enough!"

After ascending the little hill, he walked ahead and entered a forest. The plants there gave the impression that they were moving together with their leaves and vibrating, as if they were expressing joy. Daniele thought to himself, "Will not they also tell me that they are praising the Creator?" Then he heard a voice responding to his unspoken question. "Certainly! Yes, we praise the Creator!" He asked, "How, in what way do you do so?" Their reply: "With our beauty, to purify the air and provide oxygen for people, the people that are so ungrateful towards our Creator." Daniele's impression upon hearing this was that all creation is reproving mankind!

Proceeding along in the forest he encountered many animals – squirrels, birds, even a herd of elephants who made a great noise as they paraded, and as they passed by it seemed that the trees moved out of their way. Then he saw, resting on top of a rock, a majestic and beautiful lion. Although aware that the lion would not hurt him, Daniele was still afraid, and he ordered the lion not come near him. If it wanted to speak it would have to do so from where it was sitting. To the lion, he asked the same question – what is your task? And it replied in basically the same words at the fish, adding, "We can praise the Creator, but we cannot offer Him love. This is something that only people with immortal souls can do. Ah! If mankind only understood what love is! All of our praises are nothing in the face of an act of love made by a human to our Creator. And we entrust all our praises to a priest living in the world because he is so pleasing to the Most High." Daniele responded, "I understand, he is Padre Pio." Then the lion, as did the large fish, bowed profoundly upon hearing the name of Padre Pio. Daniele felt a bit of pride, because he knows and even lives with Padre Pio.

After concluding his conversations with the lion and the other animals of the forest, Fran Daniele kept walking until he came before an ancient tree. It was so large that three men would not be able to reach around its trunk. At the foot of this tree, feeling tired and dazed, he sat down in the hopes of not having to experience anything further. This plant was a type of cedar of Lebanon, whose branches did not overhang, and was almost completely stripped of its bark, remnants of which clung to the trunk. Daniele wondered if this tree too would tell him that it praises the Creator. The reply was immediate, "Certainly! Yes I do praise the Creator! I cannot love Him, but only praise Him. Indeed, and for centuries I have carried out my task. I gather all of the praises of the different plants and the trees throughout the world, and by means of a priest who, except for Jesus, is the most pleasing to God, I offer them to our Creator." Immediately Daniele said, "The priest is Padre Pio." He felt good in just pronouncing his name, since he was his personal friend.

All at once he heard rustling noises. Looking around, he saw that the ancient tree and all the other plants were bending in reverence. After having them resume their proper bearing, Daniele exhorted the ancient cedar to speak to him about Padre Pio. It spoke to Daniele for a long time about Jesus as High Priest, and then launched into a panegyric on the priesthood of Padre Pio, the man so pleasing to God, who knew how to make present the person and the message of Jesus in every way. The discourse of the ancient cedar was marvelous, and Daniele had never heard of anyone speak of Padre Pio so beautifully. Since he knew Padre Pio well, he could confirm that what he was hearing about him was truthful. Unfortunately, he can now no longer remember all the particulars, only that it was a magnificent tribute.

It was at this point that Daniele found himself sitting on his bed, wide awake. He thought to himself, "How is this possible. I was awake and yet was there, in all those places. I don't understand what happened, or what to call it. One thing I am sure of – it all really happened." Afterwards he laid down on the bed trying to make sense out of it in his mind. But the more he thought about that journey, the more mysterious it seemed. "Now I understand Saint Francis, I understand his Canticle of the Creatures: *Praised be You, my Lord, through all Your creatures.*"

The next morning, when Daniele was traveling by bus and trolley for his radiation therapy, whenever they passed by any trees, he felt he wanted to greet them, and in fact he did greet them. But he was very careful not to be noticed, otherwise people would think he was crazy.

When he returned from his treatments in Rome back to San Giovanni Rotondo, he related the entire occurrence to Padre Pio. After he listened to it all, Padre Pio said, "And so it is, my son." ("Cosi è, figlio mio.") In this way he confirmed and sealed as the truth: that all Creation converges on him and he offers everything to the Creator.

This article is based on Brother Natale's own testament of his vision, found at the website of the *Friends of Fra Natale http://www.amicidifradaniele.it/sito/*

Frank M. Rega

XXI. HE FELT THE PAINS OF PURGATORY

One day, while he was praying for the souls in Purgatory, Padre Pio saw a vision of one of those suffering persons completely enwrapped in flames. Marveling at the vigor and power of the fire, he was moved to ask the soul if that fire was hotter than flames on the earth. "Alas," replied the sorrowful creature, "All the fire on the earth compared to that of Purgatory is like a breath of fresh air." Padre Pio then asked him how such a thing could be possible. In reply, the soul in the vision invited the friar to experience it himself. Padre Pio then touched with his hand what seemed to be just a bit of sweat which fell from the forehead of the being. He immediately emitted a loud cry, and because of the great intensity of the pain, and his fear, he fell to the ground.

Hearing the shout, other friars rushed over, to assist in whatever way possible. When he came to himself, Padre Pio recounted the terrible experience, in which he was both a witness and a victim. He ended the tale with these words: "Oh, my brothers, if only each one of us knew how great is the severity of Divine Justice, we would never sin."

Late one evening at the friary in San Giovanni Rotondo, the friars suddenly heard the loud clamor of voices at the entrance-way, who were exclaiming "Viva Padre Pio!" It was during the Second World War, well after the evening repast, and the friary had already closed up for the night. Acting as if it were something of no importance, but just an everyday occurrence, Padre Pio calmly reassured his confrères. He explained that the voices shouting "Viva Padre Pio" were those of soldiers who had been killed in the fighting; they had come there to thank him for his prayers.

One day, in 1943, Padre Gerardo De Caro recommended the soul of someone recently deceased to the prayers of Padre Pio. It was the soul of an author whose works Padre Gerardo had enjoyed reading as a child. He did not mention his name to the saint, and had said nothing more about him. But Padre Pio understood perfectly to whom he was referring. His face reddened, as if he were experiencing torment, pity, and sorrow for the pains of another. He grieved for that person, for whom there had been no lack of spiritual help and prayers. Then Padre Pio said: "He loved creatures too much."

Padre Gerardo then beseeched, more with a look of anguish than with words, how long that soul would have to remain in Purgatory. The reply: "Almost a hundred years!" Padre Pio continued: "It is necessary to pray for the souls in Purgatory. It is difficult to believe just how much they can help our spiritual well being, through the gratitude that they show to those on earth who remember and pray for them."

Padre Pio's father, Grazio Forgione, would often travel from his home in Pietrelcina to visit his son for a few days at the friary in San Giovanni Rotondo. The Superior of the monastery allowed him to spend the nights in one the vacant cells. One evening in 1928, when he was about 67 years old, he took leave of the friars and his son at the close of their dinner and recreation period, and headed for his assigned room. It was cell number 10. As he walked down the hallway and approached the room, he was surprised to see two friars standing right in front of the doorway, blocking him from entering.

Grazio thought they were visiting friars who had mistakenly gone to the wrong room. He calmly began to explain to them that he had to take his rest, and asked them to let him enter, since this was his assigned cell. But it was to no avail. He repeated his request a couple of times, but the two friars held their ground, and gave no reply. Beginning to become impatient, he tried to convince them that it was not their room because it had only one bed. Finally, he decided it was time to simply force his way past the men. But as soon as he began to push his way through to his cell, the two friars just vanished into thin air!

Confused, shaken, and fearful, he immediately set off to find his son, and told him about this mysterious occurrence. Padre Pio understood right away what had happened. He put his arm around his dad's shoulder, and with gentle words comforted him until he began to calm down. When he saw that his father's fear had subsided, he told him: "Dad, these two friars that you have just seen in front of your room are two pitiable religious who are in Purgatory. They are doing their expiation here in the very place in which they had violated the rule of St. Francis. They are also asking our prayers for their liberation. Therefore, be calm and don't worry. They will not return again. Then Padre Pio accompanied his father back to cell number 10 and waited until he had gotten into bed, before bidding him good night.

Padre Giuseppe Antonio, of the friary of St. Anna in nearby Foggia, was one of Padre Pio's close friends. He was suffering greatly because of major kidney problems, and was under the watchful care of the doctors and friars. On December 30, Padre Pio was informed that the condition of Padre Antonio was worsening, and only prayers and divine intervention could alleviate his suffering and cure him.

Padre Pio did not need to be asked twice. That night in his cell, as he was praying for his desperately ill friend, there was knock on his door. "Avanti," said the Padre upon hearing the sound. The door opened and to his great surprise and wonder, Padre Antonio entered the room. Padre Pio greeted him with: "How are you doing? I was told that you were suffering from a grave illness, and now I find you here!" The friar replied, "I am doing well. All of my torments are over and I have come to thank you for your prayers." And then he disappeared. Unbeknownst to Padre Pio, Padre Antonio had died that very evening of December 30.

Carmela Marocchino lived near the friary at the house of Mary Pyle, the American who had become his disciple. Carmela's brother, Padre Vittore, was a beloved priest until his sudden death in January of 1958. Wondering if he had saved his soul, she went to Padre Pio a few days later. She began to cry, and so did Padre Pio. She asked the Padre why the Lord had taken her brother. He explained that the Lord entered a garden where there many beautiful flowers. Walking over to the most beautiful flower of all, he picked it. This is exactly what happened to Padre Vittore. Carmela then asked if her brother was saved. Padre Pio answered in the affirmative, but added that we must pray.

Some months later, hoping that Padre Vittore would now be in Paradise, she asked Padre Pio in the confessional if her brother was now in heaven. He replied, "My daughter, we priests have more responsibility before God, and when we appear before Him, it is with fear and trembling. Therefore, let us pray." Then, about a year after her brother's death, she again asked Padre Pio about him. This time his answer was, "He is in Paradise." Carmela was overjoyed. But she began to consider that even though he had been a priest, and was a student of Padre Pio's, he still had to spend 11 months in Purgatory. This was because of the responsibility of so many souls under his spiritual direction.

On yet another occasion, Carmela asked Padre Pio if she should still pray for her deceased parents. He replied, "Even if your parents are in heaven, we must always pray. If they no longer need prayers, they are applied to other souls."

One time in 1949 Padre Pio was talking with a certain doctor who was very close to him. They were discussing prayers for the dead. Padre Pio said to him, "Maybe you don't know that even now I can pray for the happy death of my great-grandfather!" But the doctor remarked that he has been dead for many, many years. Then Padre Pio explained, "For the Lord the past does not exist. Everything is an eternal present. These prayers had already been taken into account. And so I repeat that even now I can pray for the happy death of my great-grandfather!"

Based on accounts in *Padre Pio Mistero e Miracolo*, by G. Giacometti and P. Sessa, pp. 225-35, and also *The Holy Souls*, by Padre Alessio Parente, pp, 103-104 and pp. 177-179.

Frank M. Rega

XXII. HE CORRECTS A MISCHIEVOUS BOY

It happened back in 1939, when Gigino was only nine years old. Everyone at San Giovanni Rotondo called him Gigino, but his name was actually Luigi Capotosto. He lived with his parents on the Viale Cappuccini, the road which led directly to the friary and church of Santa Maria delle Grazie. One day near the Patariello, the hill upon which the friary stood, Gigino played a nasty trick on his best friend by furtively stealing his knapsack, which contained the lunch that the boy was to bring to his father at work. Just as he was about to open the satchel to partake of its contents, he saw a friar emerge from along the top of the hill – it was Padre Pio, although Gigino did not know it at the time.

Gigino, fearful that his "crime" had been discovered, tried to flee to avoid being punished, but he tripped and fell at the edge of the road, which was rugged and unpaved at the time. He scraped his knee, and as the blood ran down his leg, he saw the friar approaching him. He was terrified, because he feared the monk had found him out and was going to report him to the police. He had heard that not long ago, when a boy of his age had broken a window, the boy and his parents were summoned to the police station.

But instead, to his surprise, the friar, showing great compassion, came over to help him, and in a gentle and kind voice asked what had happened. The intensity of his eyes, the magnetic expression of his face, and a smile that invited trust and affection, induced Gigino to make a complete confession of the entire event. "I told him of the games we boys were playing and confessed that I stole the rucksack of my best friend. Then when I added that I knew that it contained his father's lunch, the monk did not have hard words for me or threaten me with punishment. Instead, with a calm voice and in a reassuring tone, he explained to me all the consequences of my action. After a hard morning's work, the father of that boy would have nothing to eat. My seemingly innocent trick has become instead an abuse of the poor worker. It was a lesson in life that, even though I learned it while so young, has remained impressed in my mind as an indelible memory throughout the years."

As he rose to his feet, Gigino noticed that the friar's hands appeared to be wrapped in cloth. He asked out of simple, childlike curiosity, if he too had fallen down. Why were his hands wrapped? The monk answered that no, he had not fallen. "These are my poor sacrifices for the Lord." Astonished, Gigino asked him who was this Lord, and Padre Pio's concise reply was "One day you will see and you will understand."

Now, as an adult, Gigino can firmly avow that those words were prophetic, because on the day of his accident, he truly understood who this Lord was. He had become a delivery truck driver, and periodically drove up the Gargano mountain from the plains below to San Giovanni Rotondo, to deliver meats and grains to various stores and other businesses. The serpentine road along the mountain-side is extremely steep, consisting of five sharp, hair-pin turns, with the edge of the road dangerously close to the cliffs with sheer drop-offs below.

One day in 1963 with Gigino driving the truck, and a co-worker sitting next to him in the cab, they began the long descent down the mountain after making their delivery run. As they were making a turn around one of the sharp bends in the road, Gigino tried to slow down the truck, when he suddenly realized that the brakes did not work. The steel control rod connecting the brake pedal to the wheel carriage had broken. He frantically tried to use the emergency brake, and to mesh the gears, but the truck just kept bounding along, swaying from left to right, going faster and faster. At any moment they could fail to round one of the hairpin turns and tumble down the escarpment. Gigino gripped the steering wheel hard, as he desperately tried to keep his vehicle on the roadway.

While his co-worker could only scream and curse, Gigino began to earnestly and fervently pray to all the saints of Paradise! They tried jumping out of the careening truck, but were afraid because of its great velocity. As they barreled down towards the next sharp turn, all at once a very intense perfume of roses penetrated the driver's cab. The aroma was so strong and instantaneous that they could only breathe with difficulty. It was the sign of Padre Pio's spiritual presence, and it seemed to suffocate them. Seconds later the speeding truck abruptly halted, amid the sound of a violent crash. It had smashed into the trunk of a giant olive tree that stood right on the edge of the curve.

"I have no image in my mind of the actual impact, we seemed to be enveloped by a protective cloud. I only recall that after some minutes had passed, we realized that we were uninjured." Gigino and his companion crawled out from the twisted and smoking wreck. Neither man had a scratch on them nor any other effects or bruises from the impact. They looked out on an incredible scene – at the apex of the hairpin turn, the olive tree overlooked a steep ravine. If they had gone over that cliff in the truck, not even their bones would have been found. If the tree were located half a meter to the left or to the right of the precipice, their lives would have been over. "Right below the driver's cab, through which the branches of the tree now protruded, we could see the wide, deep valley below. In sum, it was a miracle we were alive!"

But Gigino's special connection with Padre Pio did not end there. Oddly enough, exactly one year later he was on that same road, running the same delivery route, but this time of course in a new truck. It was raining cats and dogs, and was already dark out. He had come to the curve where he had his fortunate escape, and had just passed that same olive tree, when he saw a broken down car at the edge of the road. He saw the driver working a tire iron in the pouring rain, trying to change a flat tire. Gigino, aware of the great grace he had received at this very spot, knew that it was his duty to help out this poor man and vehicle stuck here in the cloudburst. He stopped his truck, and as he came near the auto, he saw that it bore a license plate with the letters "SCV," Stato della Citta del Vaticano, and he noticed bishop's colors on the vestments of the passenger inside. This was the car of His Excellency Karol Wojtyla, Auxiliary Bishop of Kracow, Poland, and Titular Bishop of OMBI.

It was 1964 and the Vatican Council was going full tilt. Mary Pyle, who lived practically adjacent to Padre Pio's friary, has remarked that "So many bishops from the ecumenical council came up to see Padre Pio that sometimes it seems that the Council is at San Giovanni Rotondo!" So such a private visit would not be unusual, and in the case of Bishop Wojtyla, there was a special reason for him to want to see Padre Pio and thank him in person. Two years previously the bishop had written him asking for prayers for his good friend Dr. Wanda Poltawska, who was scheduled to be operated on for late stage cancer. When it was time for the operation, the doctors were astonished to find that the tumor had disappeared.

Gigino helped change the tire, and saw to it that the car and its passenger were safely on its journey. Little could he have known, or even remotely imagined at the time, that he had helped the future Vicar of Christ, John Paul II, who would be the very pope to canonize Padre Pio.

This post is based on an account in *I Miracoli che Hanno Fatto Santo Padre Pio*, by Enrico Malatesta, pp. 176-179. Additional information from *Padre Pio the True Story* by C. Bernard Ruffin, pp. 360-361.

XXIII. PADRE PIO CROWNED WITH THORNS

At Mass, He saw Padre Pio crowned with thorns; until then he had considered him a fraud and charlatan.

While Padre Pio was still alive, there was a pious young girl who was engaged to a university student who had lost his faith, disdaining religious practices. She would not go through with marrying him unless he returned to the Church. They had argued about this incessantly but to no avail. Finally he consented to come to San Giovanni Rotondo with her, although he was quite cynical. He did not believe in the holiness of Padre Pio, considering him an impostor and charlatan.

They went to early Mass at the friary church, and on the first morning the girl was amazed to see her fiancé looking pale and shocked as he gazed at the altar during the Consecration. He whispered to her, "Does this happen every day?" She said yes, but was not aware of what he really meant by the question. This went on for a number of days.

One morning at Mass she saw him crying like a baby. Leaving the church, he explained to her that he sees Padre Pio on the altar with a knotted crown of thorns on his head, and blood running down his face. His priestly garments are illuminated by a dazzling light. He looks like the "Ecce Homo!" with his face transformed into the face of Jesus. The fiancé said he was crying because he was so moved upon seeing that in spite of all his apparent suffering, Padre Pio remained serene, sweet and peaceful. The young man thought that everyone else in the church saw the same thing.

The girl was amazed and troubled. She did not know if he was being completely truthful, or if he was suffering from an emotionally induced illusion. Thus, after she made her confession to Padre Pio, she asked the saint if her fiancé had really seen what he had told her about. He confirmed that what he had said to her was true.

The young man himself went to see Padre Pio in the sacristy. He told him that at first he saw three crowns of thorns, and then at other times what looked like a bonnet of thorns. The Padre told him, "Thank the Lord, and don't be frightened or afflicted, because I am not suffering as much as it appears," ["io non soffro quanto tu vedi"]. He asked him to speak to no one about this. "The secrets of God are to be guarded in the heart. The Lord loves you, make the effort to always be faithful to Him."

The young man in fact did not tell anyone, but it was his fiancée and relatives that spread the word. They added that the young man, when at Mass, could only see the altar and Padre Pio, and not the other people who filled the little church. Cleonice Morcaldi, a long-time spiritual daughter of Padre Pio, was a friend of the man. When Padre Alberto D'Apolito went to visit her, he met him in person, and the fiancé confirmed the truth of everything. In his book of *Memories*, Padre D'Apolito says that the name of this youth was Bruno G., and he was from Lucera, a small town not far from San Giovanni Rotondo. He writes that a few years later, Padre Pio himself married the couple, and they remained faithful to the Church.

This conversion story was told to a Polish woman staying at San Giovanni, who happened to be a painter. Inspired by the event, she painted a picture of the head of Padre Pio crowned with thorns, with his suffering face covered with blood. It was not just a circular crown, but a rough mass of thorns as if pressed down upon his head. "And that, if we think of it, is exactly how it must have been," wrote John McCaffery, who had been invited to see the painting. It was hanging on the wall of the home of Cleonice Morcaldi. The picture was covered with a kind of veil out of caution, lest someone think it presumptuous to paint Padre Pio this way, without having heard the background story behind it.

When Cleonice first heard the reports about the vision, she prayed to the Blessed Mother to assist her in finding out the truth from Padre Pio himself. One day, after confessing to him, she asked if was true that the young man saw the crown of thorns on his head. Padre Pio replied "E ne dubiti?" [And you doubt it?"], as he shut the confessional's window. In her own book about her memories of the saint, Miss Morcaldi added that some time later, she asked Padre Pio if he bore the crown of thorns outside of Mass. His reply was, "Yes, both before and afterwards." She asked which sins were expiated by Jesus by these thorns. His reply, "All of them, particularly sinful thoughts." Another time he said to Cleonice, "You must know that through Divine condescension I suffer all that Jesus suffered, his entire Passion, as much as possible for a human creature."

Based on John McCaffery's *The Friar of San Giovanni, Tales of Padre Pio,* pp 79-80; Padre Alberto D'Apolito's *Padre Pio of Pietrelcina, Memories, Experiences, Testimonials*; p. 102-103; Fr. John A. Schug's *A Padre Pio Profile,* pp. 92-93; and Cleonice Morcaldi's *La Mia Vita Vicino a Padre Pio*, Chapter 3.

XXIV. PADRE PIO HITCHES A RIDE

Bilocation does not exclude ordinary means of transportation.

In the autumn of 1949 a young man was in the Boston area, working at Harvard University for the purpose of scientific research. He was preparing for a trip by auto to visit Ottawa, Canada. While at Harvard he had become acquainted with an elderly descendant of Italian immigrants who, like many Italian-Americans, was quite attracted to the homeland of his ancestors. That man, whose name was John, was a restorer of paintings, and had done some restorations for pictures belonging to a bishop living in Ottawa. Consequently, John asked the younger man if he would be so kind as to deliver the cleaned and restored paintings to the good bishop. The researcher replied that was no trouble at all for him to do so.

After driving to Ottawa, he went straight to the

bishop's residence to bring him the renewed artwork. The bishop received the visitor into his study, and the two men engaged in polite conversation. There was a photo on the prelate's desk, which attracted the attention of the visitor, since it looked like a picture of Padre Pio. The bishop confirmed that it was indeed Padre Pio, and that he had become a disciple and great admirer of him, after meeting him in Italy during the course of the war. The face of Padre Pio was familiar to the Harvard researcher, since his mother was quite devoted to him.

During their conversation, the bishop had told him that unfortunately there were no Capuchin friars or convents at all in Ottawa. Therefore one can imagine this visitor's surprise and troubled amazement, when, upon exiting the court-yard of the bishopric, he came face to face with a Capuchin! The monk bore an uncanny resemblance to Padre Pio himself. The researcher stood amazed as the friar spoke to him with a strong southern Italian accent, and asked for a ride to the home of an acquaintance who was urgently awaiting his arrival. Dumbfounded, he signaled to the friar to get into his car, which was parked nearby. As they rode along, he followed the directions given by the monk (keep to the right . . . turn left here), without saying a word himself.

In a short time they arrived at their destination. Thanking the man with a "Pace e bene" (peace and good), the friar exited the car and all but ran up the four steps to the doorway of a house, into which he was quickly admitted. Still emotionally disoriented, the driver left his car and began to pace back and forth along the sidewalk, mulling over his extraordinary experience. For what seemed like an hour or more he waited for the friar to come back outside; but there was no sign of him.

Finally, he climbed up the steps and knocked on the door of the home. He was greeted by an older woman who seemed upset, but at the same time was smiling. Before he could utter a word, she told him, "The Padre already left a while ago. But my husband is now serenely at rest in the peace of the Lord. Padre Pio accompanied him to Paradise." The driver said goodbye to the woman, and returned to his automobile disquieted and confused.

About half an hour later he stopped at a motel to spend the night there. On the pillow of the bed he found a small sheet of paper. On it he read, "Thank you again, well done." One can imagine his bewildered state. He folded the piece of paper into his wallet; but some months later it completely disappeared, and he was unable to find it.

Then two years later, in 1951, he returned to Italy and found the time to make a brief visit to San Giovanni Rotondo. He waited as Padre Pio made his way through the throng of the faithful. As soon as the saint saw him, Padre Pio blessed him and asked if he had made a good journey back home from Canada.

Based upon an account in *Padre Pio Mistero e Miracolo*, by G. Giacometti and P. Sessa, pp. 131-132. The authors never give the actual name of the protagonist.

XXV. THE DOUBTING THOMAS

It was January of 1931 when Ubaldo Giovanni from Bologna read about Padre Pio for the first time. The wonders of the saint were related in a booklet written by Alberto Del Fante, who was one of the very first authors to write about the stigmatist and mystic from San Giovanni Rotondo. Ubaldo was a practicing Catholic, but was rather skeptical about some of the stories of the cures, conversions and miracles he had just read about. He placed the booklet where his father could find and read it when he returned from work. Later, when his father, Gattamorta, had finished reading it, Ubaldo asked him, "Doesn't it seem to you, dad, that these stories about Padre Pio are rather exaggerated? Personally, I am like St. Thomas, there are some things that if I do not experience them first hand, I just don't believe them. For that reason I would love to make a trip to San Giovanni Rotondo."

And so Gattamorta, Ubaldo, his cousin Narda, and a few friends and relatives, decided to make the trip to see Padre Pio for themselves. Then with their own eyes they could see if these many tales and stories were true. Thus on the 12th of February, they departed Bologna and headed for San Giovanni Rotondo in the south of Italy. They arrived there about noon, and at about 4:00 pm went into the monastery for Confession. Afterwards, Ubaldo's father later wrote that, to be truthful, when he made his confession, Padre Pio did not make any particular impression on him, and the same was true of the other people in the group from Bologna.

The very next day, they all went to the friary again for Communion. Afterwards, when Padre Pio entered the sacristy, they went up one by one to kiss his hand. Ubaldo and the other Bolognese with him experienced a very strong and extraordinary odor of perfume when they did so. However, they marveled when Ubaldo's father Gattamorta said he had not smelled anything, even though they insisted that it was very strong. Every day during their trip, whenever they came up to Padre Pio to kiss his stigmatized hand, they could smell the same perfume. However, Gattamorta only smelled it one time, and it happened when he was in the church, but not with Padre Pio. The aroma was on his hands, and when he approached the others, they told him it was the exact same perfume that they had all experienced.

Notwithstanding the experience of the perfume,

Ubaldo still retained his skepticism, while his father had no difficulty in accepting the truth about Padre Pio's sanctity. Then one day, while they were walking up the road leading to the friary, an idea flashed through Gattamorta's mind. He would pray for something to occur that would prove Padre Pio's powers even to his son.

They reached the friary and church, and the little group knelt before the altar waiting to receive Communion, which was distributed by Padre Pio after Mass. When it was Ubaldo's turn, he held the paten in his hand. Suddenly, he turned pale and waxen like a candle, let go of the paten, and started to fall backwards. His father rushed over to him and held him tightly in his arms. Ubaldo's body seemed cold as marble, and to Gattamorta it seemed that his son had no signs of life.

Assisted by Ubaldo's cousin Narda, they brought him into the sacristy and seated him on a bench, where he remained immobile. They sprayed water on his face, and someone found some vinegar which they put under his nose, but nothing could revive him. When Padre Pio had finished his Mass and went into the sacristy, Ubaldo was still in this state. What was the Padre's reaction upon seeing him? First he smiled at him kindly and gently. Then he put his hand upon his head and lovingly caressed his head and face. At this, Ubaldo suddenly revived.

His father began to cry after witnessing his son coming to life again upon the touch of Padre Pio. Gattamorta asked him if he felt ill, but Ubaldo replied that he did not feel sick at all. He expressed a desire to receive Communion when Padre Pio returned to the chapel to distribute it, and both father and son went to receive the Holy Particle from the saint's stigmatized hand. Afterwards in the sacristy, Padre Pio once again gave a gentle caress to Ubaldo, and kissed him on the forehead.

Throughout the rest of that day, Ubaldo felt completely well. He remained so for the duration of their stay at San Giovanni Rotondo and also after their return home to Bologna. It was the first time something like this had ever happened to him, and it was also the last time. After his encounters with Padre Pio, Ubaldo became his enthusiastic admirer, and his devoted spiritual child.

Not long after their homecoming, a telegram arrived for Ubaldo's cousin Narda, who was at that time living in the same home with Gattamorta's family. His father Giacomo, was the brother-in-law of Gattamorta. With a few words, the telegram stated that Narda's father was gravely ill and he wanted to see his son. "Giacomo grave, attendo Narda." As soon as he read the cryptic message, Narda burst out crying, fearing that his father might be dying. Ubaldo and Narda immediately left for Ravenna to the home of the sick man. Upon seeing him, Ubaldo urgently wired Gattamorta stating that Uncle Giacomo was very sick, stricken by cerebrospinal meningitis. His condition was hopeless.

The attending doctor, a noted Ravenna physician, told the family, "I do not want to delude you, your father is more dead than alive. Speak to him now about anything you wish to tell him, because it may only be a matter of hours. There is absolutely no hope that he can survive more than four days at the most."

But Narda had with him a picture of Padre Pio. Placing the picture under the pillow of his father, he began praying to the stigmatized friar. The very next day, the doctor returned and to his surprise found his patient sitting up in bed on his own. The physician declared, "They say that miracles are a thing of the past, but to me it seems that they still can occur!"

Then after only one more day, Giacomo was able to leave his bed.

When Narda and his sisters met with the doctor to thank him, his reply was, "Do not thank me, since I have done nothing, and no other doctor could have done anything either. What happened I do not know, perhaps it was the Lord or his Mother. It is certain that, of the people in your father's condition who are hospitalized, few manage to survive, and they never fully recover.

They are either blind, or deaf, or mentally incapacitated. But Giacomo regained his complete health in a few days."

As for Giacomo, he shows the picture of Padre Pio to everyone he can, and proclaims, "My son Narda says that this is the image of the friar that cured me!"

Based on an account in *Per La Storia*, by Alberto Del Fante, pp. 348-352.

XXVI. PADRE PIO SAVED HIS LIFE

Padre Pio saved Michele's life during World War II, but then refused to hear his confession.

Michele Cardone was born in Padre Pio's hometown of Pietrelcina, before moving to Australia later in his life. While he was living in Italy, he heard Padre Pio spoken of often, even from his childhood. However, he never bothered to find out anything about the saint, and was not even sure what he looked like. As a young adult, all he knew about him was that he was a holy monk who lived in San Giovanni Rotondo.

When the Second World War broke out, Michele volunteered for the Navy, and was assigned to various ships. On Palm Sunday, April 18, 1943, he was serving on board the destroyer Alpino, which was anchored at the port of La Spezia, in northern Italy. The chaplain of the ship had invited the sailors to perform their Easter duty that morning, by going to confession and communion. Almost everyone responded to the request, except for a few. Among those few was Michele Cardone. But it was not because he was opposed or indifferent to the sacraments. Instead, during his next shore leave, he was planning on going home to Pietrelcina, and then from there to travel to San Giovanni Rotondo, in order to make his confession to Padre Pio, and to receive communion from him. It was to be his first visit to see him and his friary.

But that Palm Sunday evening, about half an hour before midnight, an alarm suddenly sounded, taking the 200-man crew by surprise. A heavy incursion of enemy aircraft rumbled overhead, and they began raining down their load of bombs. In just a few minutes, the earth and the sky were transformed into an immense ring of light and fire, both from the anti-aircraft artillery and from the exploding projectiles. There were enormous flames and deafening booms – it seemed like the end of the world. The destroyer Alpino was directly hit by the incendiary bombs at many points, causing deaths and injuries among the crew. The ship began to take on water through the numerous holes opened by the bombs, and slowly began to sink. In the meantime, crude oil naphtha began leaking from damaged storage tanks on board; it ignited and spread in rivulets of fire along the deck.

The sailors were trying to remain calm as the situation became more frightening, but the terror disoriented everyone completely. They did not know where to go to seek safety because of the suffocating fumes and heat produced by the spread of the burning naphtha. In addition, munitions that were stored on the deck were beginning to explode due to the intense heat, endangering the larger ammunition stores that were below deck in the interior of the ship. The situation was desperate. In those moments Michele was sure that his life would be over.

"Then I beheld before me, at some distance, the figure of a monk with a beard, who had suddenly appeared. He was there with his arms opened wide as if waiting for someone at the opposite side of the quay. I don't know why, but I regained courage and hope again." Then, just as quickly as he had emerged, the monk disappeared. How would it be possible to get across through the flames of the naphtha raging on the ship and on the dock? "Then I saw once again above and in front of me the same friar beckoning me with open, inviting arms. I became infused with tremendous energy, and dragging along with me two wounded companions, succeeded in reaching a place of safety."

A few days after that fearful April night, all of the uninjured survivors were allowed a short period of leave. Michele returned to his home in Pietrelcina, in order to be reunited with his family, and to refresh himself spiritually and physically. He hastened to the parish church of Our Lady of the Angels, to make his thanksgiving before the statue of the Madonna della

Libera (Our Lady Liberatrix), the Patron Saint of Pietrelcina, to whom Padre Pio was very devoted. Then on the first of May, Michele, accompanied by his mother, traveled to San Giovanni Rotondo. They entered the monastery church, where he waited in line to confess to Padre Pio. "While I was waiting for my turn to make by confession, I began to feel empty and spiritually dry in my soul. When my turn arrived, and I saw Padre Pio for the very first time, my breath was taken away, and my heart gave a start. He resembled perfectly the monk whom I had seen two times in front of me with open arms during the evening of the bombardment at La Spezia."

But Padre Pio refused to hear his confession. Brushing him away he said to Michele, "One does not pray to God only at San Giovanni Rotondo!" Although mortified and confused, the very next morning Michele returned to the friary. This time Padre Pio listened with kindness to his confession. His emotions reached a peak when later he was allowed to visit the saint in his cell. Padre Pio blessed him, saying, "Go forward, pray, and may God be with thee."

Based on Michele Cardone's account in the magazine "Voce di Padre Pio," January 1996, page 46.

XXVII. AT THE THRESHOLD OF PARADISE

Maria Castro of Santiago, Chile is a graphic designer who volunteers and collaborates in the work of evangelizing. She had prayed to the Heavenly Father and to the Blessed Virgin to be permitted to work exclusively for the Church. It was 2004, and at this time Maria was very happy with her life, so much so that she thought that her joy might be too good to be true. When she prayed to the Blessed Virgin, she would say, "It is not possible I could be so happy. You must be preparing something, you have something in store for me."

Maria and her collaborators decided to seek for testimonies of miracles, and interviewed people who had received such favors through the intercession of the Blessed and Saints of Chile. She also wished to collect testimonies from any who had knowledge of miracles from Padre Pio, but in Chile she was only able to find one such case. However, the person did not wish to be interviewed about it. After she was denied an interview about the Padre Pio miracle, she prayed to him, saying she was sorry that she could not find any testimonies, therefore he would have to be excluded from the collection of miracle stories.

The very next day, she began to feel quite cold. She was not too concerned, thinking that it was just a passing sickness. But soon there were days when she had trouble even getting out of bed. She began to take various medicines, and was easily fatigued by the simplest tasks. She became tormented by a constant headache and shivering, and started to lose her voice.

After she developed a low grade fever, and had difficulty swallowing, her husband drove her to the hospital. The doctors were unsure of a diagnosis, but she was admitted as a precaution, and was provided with an oxygen mask. Her husband went home, and then returned with some of her personal items, including a bible and a book about Padre Pio that she had intended to read. He also affixed a picture of Padre Pio with a novena prayer over the headboard of Maria's hospital bed. After further tests and x-rays, the doctors concluded that she had severe pneumonia with acute respiratory insufficiency. Lesions had formed inside of her mouth, making it very difficult for her to speak; she could only eat jelly-like food, and had to be given water intravenously.

That night she had to remain almost in a sitting position in bed, with her mask on, and had been injected with antibiotics. She prayed to Padre Pio, and offered her sickness and suffering to God in reparation for attacks against the Church, for the Holy Father Pope John Paul II, and for the bishops. But she began to think that perhaps the Lord might not be content with her modest offering, and therefore she requested of Padre Pio: "If it is necessary that I suffer more, please tell the Lord that I am ready." She recalled that he had asked people to send him their guardian angel, and she did so. She sent her angel with a message confirming her offer to suffer. It would not be long before she became aware that Padre Pio had received the message.

Because of the discomfort of the oxygen mask, she could not get to sleep. The clock showed that it was two thirty in the morning. Suddenly she had a great desire to confess her most serious sins. She prayed that Padre Pio would find her a confessor as soon as she left the hospital, a priest whom she could confess to as if he were Padre Pio himself.

Almost immediately she saw next to her bed an apparition of a confessional made of wood. She was still completely awake, and was not delirious or feverish. A middle-aged slightly overweight priest with blondish hair entered the confessional, and asked her to begin recounting her sins. She confessed everything she could remember, saving the worst for last. At that point there was a loud noise, and the priest pointed out to Maria something to her left.

She looked where he was pointing and saw with her own eyes Padre Pio himself next to her bed. "He looked at me with an expression of indescribable tenderness, while giving me absolution with his right hand. This was no apparition or phantasm: he had a solid human body, which even projected a shadow!" She was still wearing the mask, and could barely speak, so she kept whispering, "Padre Pio, Padre Pio, Padre Pio, I love you, I do not wish to disturb you." Smiling sweetly, he nodded his head twice.

Maria wanted to reach out and touch him, but she resisted the impulse. She did not want him to think that she doubted his presence, as the Apostle Thomas. She wanted to embrace him, but did not feel she was worthy. She could not take her eyes off him: he wore a coffee-colored Capuchin habit, had the bearing and beauty of a celestial figure, strong and imposing, and seemed to be about sixty. His hands were uncovered, and there was no trace of the stigmata on them. (This is not surprising, since at the time of his death, about 35 years prior to this incident, the stigmata had completely disappeared from his body.) Padre Pio bent down and kissed her forehead with great tenderness. Within her soul she heard these words: "I have come because you have wished it. I have loved you all of your life, my daughter."

Suddenly Padre Pio removed her oxygen mask, and Maria was able to smell an intense perfume of flowers. "Then he put his left hand on my abdomen, and his right on my shoulder, and raised my body vertically up to the ceiling with incredible speed. I remained suspended in the air for three or four seconds with my arms crossed." When she came back down, he said to her, "I am very satisfied because you have not asked anything for yourself; I accept your offer. You will suffer a little more, but it will be a momentary thing, and this disease will never affect you again." Padre Pio continued looking at her. Then Maria heard a choir of angels singing praises to the Lord. She immediately sensed within her heart this message: "For you the time of man is over, and the time of God begins."

That evening her husband Roberto and her father visited her at the hospital. She was anxious to tell them of her experience and asked for a pencil. On a sheet of paper she wrote: "At about three in the morning Padre Pio came to see me." The two men exchanged a look of amazement, because they knew she was not capable of fabricating a story like that.

On the next day, her condition worsened. Another chest x-ray confirmed the prior diagnosis, "severe pneumonia with acute respiratory insufficiency." Then it was determined that one of her lungs had collapsed. She was moved to the intensive care unit, and a breathing tube was inserted in her mouth. Her husband was extremely anxious, but he was only permitted to see her for five minutes. Crying, he implored her to her not to leave him alone with two small children to care for. "Roberto believed that Padre Pio had actually visited me, but feared that he had come in order to take me away with him forever." In the meantime the doctors had become pessimistic, thinking that she might need to be hospitalized for a month. It was May 25, Padre Pio's birthday. "Surely he desired, as a birthday gift, that I offer my sufferings to the Lord."

The following morning, the x-rays revealed that her other lung had collapsed. However, towards noon she inexplicably began to respond to her therapy. She was even able to sit in an armchair. In the evening Roberto told her that her friends had offered a Mass for her healing, and her name was included in the recitation of the Rosary on Radio Maria.

On the morning of May 27, the examining Pulmonologist was surprised at her clear improvement. When he returned at midday, he exclaimed that her progress was incredible. And by evening, he was stunned, and told her that yesterday she had been in grave condition. "Do you know what I mean when I say grave?" She nodded her head, thinking of Padre Pio.

A few days later, on June 1, she was dismissed

from the hospital. Her lungs were completely healthy and the pneumonia had totally gone away. The doctor avowed that no one would believe that her before and after x-rays were from the same person! Later she learned that in her medical records at the hospital there were various questions regarding her healing, which was inexplicable for science.

From Maria's own testimony: "Today, in a time in which almost no one listens to the voice of the Church, and they point their fingers at the priests because of the grave errors of some of them, I believe that Padre Pio has manifested himself to aid us. Faithful to Jesus and the Church, he constantly suffered for everyone. He prayed without ceasing, offering himself as a victim for all of humanity. Now that he is at the threshold of Paradise, he is awaiting the arrival of his spiritual children to the very last one."

Based on an account in *Padre Pio, Miracoli Sconosciuti del Santo con le Stigmate*, by José Zavala, pp. 108-115.

XXVIII. THE GREAT EASTER MIRACLE

Paolina was gravely ill, with relatives and friends preparing for her death, but Padre Pio promised that during his Easter Mass she would rise with Christ.

In the early months of 1925, Paolina Preziosi, a holy woman and a good mother to her five children, fell ill with bronchitis. She was a Third Order Franciscan and well-liked by the people of San Giovanni Rotondo, where she lived. It was said of her that "she had a delicacy of conscience as rare and precious as her surname."

As Holy Week approached, her condition became grave, and developed into pneumonia, but there was little the attending doctor could do. Difficult days lie ahead for Paolina. Her husband Lorenzo and the children became more and more upset as she grew visibly worse. Some of her friends approached Padre

Pio to ask his help. But he replied: "What can I do, I am just a poor sinner". He added that they must pray and keep on praying, so that the Lord does not take her. Her family, relatives, friends and neighbors did pray, but it seemed that their pleas were not reaching heaven. As her condition became increasingly desperate, the doctor began to fear for her life. Medicines had no effect, and she had almost stopped eating.

On Palm Sunday, her friends once more entreated Padre Pio. They recounted their fears for the fate of her five children if she were taken away from them. But he appeared preoccupied, as if he were not sure that Divine Providence would intervene. It seemed he felt that her destiny was already decided and could not be changed. The friends continued to persist: "Padre, the doctor says there is no hope." Finally he came back to himself, and looked at them serenely, almost as if he had found a solution. Then he said to them decisively, "Paolina will rise with Jesus. She is such good person that the Lord wants her with Him in heaven, but her children need her. She must keep on praying and not be afraid. Tell her that she will rise again with the Lord."

The words of Padre Pio assumed a prophetic significance, since he was announcing a miracle to occur at a specific time. "Padre Pio said Paolina will rise with the Lord," the people repeated all during Holy Week. The news circulated throughout San Giovanni and even to neighboring towns in the province of Puglia, igniting disputes and discussions. The enemies of Padre Pio laughed, and awaited the day when the stupidity of those who believed in him would be confirmed. But others were certain that she would be cured; however, they wondered if the cure would occur at the Mass on Holy Saturday, or on Sunday.

The evening of Good Friday, the hapless woman continued to beg God to permit her to live for the sake of her children. Then Padre Pio, who was aware of her intense appeals, and was deeply moved, appeared to her in bilocation. "Do not fear," he told her. "Do not fear, child of God, have faith and hope; at Mass tomorrow, when the church bells sound for Christ's Resurrection, you will be cured."

The poor woman prayed all night, along with her friends, neighbors and relatives. They had already prepared the coffin, as was the custom in the area, since only a miracle could save her life. There was nothing doctors could do for her, because science was powerless to restore health to someone who was more dead than alive. Padre Pio, however, insisted they must continue praying to the Lord for her cure. But later that night she became comatose, and the Third Order members readied their Franciscan burial shroud, to clad her as soon as she passed.

Early in the morning on Holy Saturday, one of

her relatives, with two of Paolina's children, went to the monastery in order to once again plead with Padre Pio, who was their last hope. In the face of their unbridled tears, especially of the little ones, he could not resist their request and he redoubled his prayers. "Heavenly Father, please grant that the Sacrifice of the Mass will renew the life and health of your worthy daughter. In her goodness she is ready to be with You, but permit her to remain here upon the earth for the sake of her five young children." He embraced the two children who were present, pressing them close to himself. He was heartbroken by their innocent suffering.

In the meantime a note was passed to him, indicating that the parish priest had arrived at the Preziosi home to administer the last rites of the Church. As the morning progressed, he received further updates: she doesn't recognize anybody; she is practically dead. Then after hearing confessions, Padre Pio donned his priestly vestments. He approached the altar and began the Easter Mass for Saturday in the monastery church of Our Lady of Grace. All eyes were on him. "He is sorrowful," some said. "He has been crying," said others. "I have never seen him so downcast." But at the Gloria, everyone saw him transfigured, as large tears fell from his eyes. At the same time, the church bells, which had been silent all week, announced the Resurrection of Christ, ringing out their hosannas to the Lord! Glory to God who has risen!

At the sound of the bells, Paolina Preziosi, as if impelled by a superhuman force, rose up from her bed. She lifted up to God and to Padre Pio prayers of praise and thanksgiving and gratitude. Her fever had disappeared, and her body had returned to life, with a vitality that neither medicine nor science were capable of returning to her. To the astonishment of everyone she was completely well.

People ran outside, shouting "Miracle! Paolina is cured!" The news reverberated everywhere, even reaching those who were at Mass. "The miracle has happened," they whispered one to another, while tears streamed down their faces. At the termination of the ceremony, so many people pushed into the sacristy to see Padre Pio that the carabinieri had to intervene to curb the enthusiasm of the crowd.

Afterwards, someone remarked to him that perhaps God had wanted this woman to be with Him, but now she has come back to earth. Padre Pio replied: "It is also beautiful to be exiled from Paradise because of love!"

This mother of many children had obtained grace from the Mother of God. Padre Pio had prayed to Jesus and Saint Joseph, but in a special way to the Blessed Virgin. Certainly the phrase written over the entrance to one of the cells of his monastery must have come to his mind:

Frank M. Rega

"Mary is the entire reason for my hope."

(Maria e' tutta la ragione della mia speranza.)

This chapter is based on the original account researched by Alberto Del Fante for his book *Per La Storia*, pp. 310-312; with additional information from *Padre Pio Il Santo dei Miracoli* by Renzo Allegri, pp. 197-200.

XXIX. THE POWER OF HIS RELIC

The Honorable Giovanni Tamponi was a district magistrate in the prefecture of Cagliari on the island of Sardinia. He became one of Padre Pio's most devoted spiritual children, thanks to the saint's miraculous cure of his five-year-old son, whom he snatched from almost certain death in 1970.

The first time Giovanni had ever heard of Padre Pio was in 1958, in an article in the Catholic magazine Famiglia Christiana. In it he learned that this priest bore the wounds of Christ, and lived in a monastery in San Giovanni Rotondo on the Italian mainland. One thing struck him in particular in the article: when Padre Pio distributed Communion to the faithful, who would kneel before the altar to receive it from his hands, there were times when he refused to give someone the Host. Giovanni thought to himself: "How can a priest give the Sacred Host to some and not to others? What would he know? How can he behave this way and take on this responsibility in public?"

Desiring to learn more about this man of the cloth, within a month Signore Tamponi was on his way to San Giovanni, arriving on a cold November afternoon. By "chance," the first person he encountered in the piazza of Padre Pio's church of Santa Maria delle Grazie, was an attorney from Milan who offered to share his rented accommodations. Giovanni took this as a sign from Providence, to encourage him on his quest to know more about the Padre.

The two men rose at 4:00 am in order to arrive at the church before 5:00 when the doors would open. Giovanni, unfamiliar with the rush of the "holy women," was swept away by the crowd, which actually pushed him close to the altar. There was a sudden hush when Padre Pio appeared and the Mass began, and the silence that followed allowed him to participate in the Eucharist "in a way that is not easy to describe." Giovanni had a personal question he wanted to ask the saint, so when Mass ended he waited for him in the corridor that he traversed in order to enter the Convento. But all at once a crowd of devotees invaded the area, and he was almost swept away again. However, he was able to reach out and touch Padre Pio. He asked him the question that he had prepared beforehand, but Padre Pio brusquely said, "What do you want?" ("Che vuoi?") and just continued walking. Giovanni tried to follow but it was useless because of all the people.

His new friend, the lawyer from Milan, saw what had occurred and encouraged him to try once more later in the afternoon. So he waited at the corridor and again asked Padre Pio his question, but the saint one more time said "Che vuoi?" However, by this time Giovanni had learned how to make his way through the crowd, and was able to follow him right to the entrance door to the Convento. Padre Pio was about to disappear behind the door, when he suddenly stopped and turned towards Giovanni. Looking him right in the eye, he repeated a third time "Che vuoi?" Now the two of them were face to face, alone. Giovanni attempted to repeat his question, but was not able to utter a thing.

Then a good-natured and paternal smile opened on the Padre's seraphic face. It was a prelude to the reply that Giovanni had so much longed to hear, and this personal advice was immediately and precisely given to him. Giovanni was overcome, and realized at that instant that he was standing before no ordinary person. Padre Pio's answer was a turning point in his life, marking a fundamental milestone. He left the church overflowing with profound emotion and joy, and encountered his friend from Milan, who shared in the happiness that he had finally spoken with Padre Pio. However, after less than two full days in San Giovanni Rotondo, he had to hasten to return to his home. There his relatives and friends were preparing a celebration for his successful triumph in the exam to enter the magistracy in Italy. All during his trip back, from Puglia to the Roman port of Civitavecchia, overnight on the boat to Sardinia, and then another hour to his home town, thoughts of Padre Pio occupied his mind. The joy of passing the exam took a back seat to his enthusiasm for having met the priest that everyone was talking about, the stigmatized friar who had clearly pointed out the direction his life should take. "Already, from this first short encounter with Padre Pio, I had the definite sensation of finding myself before something truly great, of an elevated spirituality in direct contact with the Divine, of a true faith with a supernatural aura, through which I felt already protected and attracted."

The next year Giovanni Tamponi returned to San Giovanni Rotondo, and this time he was able to stay longer. Reservations were needed to confess to Padre Pio, and his turn did not come up until the fourth day of his stay. He had been going to the 5:00 am Mass, and afterwards talked to people who had confessed to the Padre. Many told him that Padre Pio recounted sins committed during their lives that they had totally forgotten about. These seemed to be mature and honest people, and Giovanni had no reason to doubt what they were saying. Having no experience with such a confessor, he was shaken and anxious as he awaited his first confession with the saint, although he felt prepared for it.

Padre Pio confessed the men in a corner of the

sacristy of the old church, behind a curtain, and furnished only with a chair and a kneeler. As his turn approached, all of his preparations became completely useless. Events and episodes of his life came to mind that he had not even considered. " I felt my mind burning and inside my soul a tumult of different feelings, of anxieties, of tensions, of agitation, of fears. I had the impression and sensation of having to be present not at a normal confession – which I was used to – but rather at a 'divine judgment'. It seemed that Padre Pio was already scrutinizing and analyzing me." He began to sweat and could not calm down, and had to loosen his tie because he felt suffocated.

Finally it was his turn, and he quickly drew the curtain and knelt before Padre Pio. They were face to face, eye to eye. "I looked at him but could not sustain his gaze; his large, black eyes penetrated into the depths of my soul." Giovanni started to mention a certain sin, but Padre Pio interrupted him, "You have already confessed that! Continue on," he urged. He conducted what was essentially an interrogation, punctuated by an occasional comment. "I experienced a fear and emotion that I cannot to this day describe." When the confession ended, he asked to be accepted as his spiritual child, and Padre Pio consented but set a certain condition.

Giovanni went into the church to pray, feeling like a different person. As a young magistrate he had sustained examinations of all types, but never had he suffered and at the same time rejoiced in any to this measure. But how did Padre Pio know that he had confessed that sin? Evidently he could read souls and saw that there was no corresponding stain on it. Giovanni stayed in town for another week, and returned to Sardinia with a much clearer picture of Padre Pio and also of his own spiritual path. Many years passed during which he continued to visit San Giovanni Rotondo. Then in 1966, during his confession to the saint, he asked him for a special blessing for his son Mario, who had just had his first birthday. Padre Pio condescended, "but perhaps in that same moment he understood that in four years time it would take a lot more than a benediction to save the boy's life."

The child was affected with a chronic urinary tract infection. He was often hospitalized but unfortunately a cause could not be determined; yet his blood nitrogen counts continued to rise. He began to visibly waste away. Finally in 1970 a prominent urologist determined that Mario suffered from a congenital malformation. His kidney function was impaired because of swollen and twisted ureters that caused urine stagnation and reflex. The only solution was a risky procedure which entailed life-threatening surgery. The boy was operated on, the malformed ureters were removed, and were substituted by a complex intestinal loop between the renal pelvis and bladder.

"The following days were terrible – the fear

about the good outcome of of such a difficult and complex intervention, on his little body already so debilitated, made us suffer profoundly." Soon it became evident that there was a serious complication: there was a blockage, an occlusion somewhere, and nothing could flow through the intestine. Therefore, no food or water could be given to little Mario. Hour by hour the situation grew graver and more critical. "On the boy there was a sad and deep expression, an indescribable thinness, an almost total absence of energy, that framed his cadaverous pallor." There was nothing that could be done except wait for the sorrowful outcome.

The family had been praying all the while, and continued to pray, but without success. Medical science was powerless to do anything, and the end seemed inevitable. Around midnight, after over a week had passed since the operation, Giovanni's wife suggested applying a Padre Pio relic of the first-class (pertaining to the physical remains of a saint) to her son. They had a clipping of linen stained with his blood. With it, Giovanni lightly and gently touched Mario' stomach, while saying the words: "Padre Pio, if you don't put your hands here, who else can do it?" As soon as he finished pronouncing these words, the boy let out a shout, "Enough!" At that same instant, a strong, rapid noise, sounding like water and compressed air together, could be heard coming from Mario's intestines, at the spot where the relic had been placed. The sound seemed to go the from center of his stomach in the direction of his bladder. Giovanni's immediate reaction was to remark: "Is this Heaven's answer?"

Mario was given a glass of water, which he was able to drink without consequences. During the entire night, the sounds of the movement of water and air persisted, as if to indicate that the intestines were resuming their normal function. At one point, Giovanni asked his son why he had shouted "Enough!" Mario replied "Papa, as soon as you touched me I felt force so strong that I could not take it any more, and I said "enough" so that you would not touch me again." And yet, Giovanni had only lightly applied the relic to the boy's stomach. "Simply from the mere contact with the relic, a mysterious power was evidently unleashed which the boy could not abide, and an internal surge breached the blockage." Only a few days later, Mario was dismissed from the hospital.

The next year, his family took Mario to the tomb of Padre Pio at the Church of *Our Lady of Grace* (Santa Maria delle Grazie), to offer their thanksgivings to the saint. Then in 1974 he made his First Holy Communion in the crypt of the same church. His father, the magistrate Giovanni Tamponi, reflecting on the miracle, noted that as soon as he had invoked the name of Padre Pio, the grace was conceded instantaneously and definitively. "Padre Pio was and is my point of reference, and after this event, how can I have doubts about his paternal care, especially now that he is so close to that Christ that he loved, served and honored so much during his life. He certainly was right when he asked one of his spiritual children to pray that the Lord would call him to heaven, because he would be able to do much more from there than he can do on earth."

This story is based on a chapter from *I Miracoli che Hanno Fatto Santo Padre Pio*, by Enrico Malatesta, pp. 374-383.

Frank M. Rega

XXX. HE SAW JESUS IN PADRE PIO

Padre Pio had personally asked Brother Daniele Natale to be his spiritual child, and perhaps this was the source of Daniele's great confidence in him. As his spiritual father, Padre Pio was always close to Daniele, who would feel the saint's loving presence even after the death of the Padre. Because of his great love and confidence in him, Daniele would sometimes approach him with intimate and unusual requests, that others would not dare to ask for. One day he showed a friend a photo, taken by another Brother, of him kissing Padre Pio's Franciscan habit on the chest, near his heart. As they looked at the picture, Fra Daniele told his friend of the time Padre Pio had desired to give him a certain, wonderful gift.

One night, it was about three in the morning, Padre Pio came unexpectedly to see Daniele in his room in the monastery where he slept. Out of the blue, Padre Pio suddenly said to him, "So! Ask me whatever you want, whatever is most dear to your heart." Daniele began to ponder what he should ask for, since he really did not need anything. Then he told Padre Pio that what he wants is to be united with him in everything. Padre Pio replied, "But I have already told you this: where you are, there I will be; where you go, there I will go. Ask me for something else." Daniele answered that this is enough for him. If Padre Pio is with him, he has everything.

However, the Padre insisted, "Ask me something else." Then, as if he had gathered his courage, Daniele said, "Father, I have a great desire to kiss your heart." Padre Pio, after leaning his chest towards him, said, "And so, kiss me!" Fra Daniele replied, "Father, I have kissed you that way hundreds and hundreds of times, what I want is to actually kiss you on your heart itself!" And Padre Pio said, "Oh I understand – you are Daniele, the man of desires."

Then Padre Pio unbuttoned his habit, lifted his undershirt, and lowered the band that kept in place the cloth that covered his heart wound. He had received this wound decades earlier, on August 5, 1918, when he was granted the mystical gift of the transverberation by means of an angel. With two fingers in the shape of scissors, the Padre laid bare the lesion. Seeing the wound on his heart, which was open and about the length of a finger, Daniele could not bring himself to kiss it. He thought to himself, "Who could have the courage to kiss it now?"

But Padre Pio, with his free hand, took Brother Daniele's head and guided it to his wounded heart, and Daniele began to kiss it. He kissed while feeling both anxiety and love, and did not want to separate himself from the Padre. "I felt within the depths of my soul something marvelous that I do not know how to describe. I was in a state of grace and breathed a most intense perfume. I felt his heart bubbling – a gurgle of blood that sounded like a small fountain from which a little stream of water rippled. I felt all this and meanwhile I continued to kiss."

After a short time Daniele stopped kissing the wound, and he looked up at Padre Pio in order to thank him. But a remarkable and beautiful sight kept him entranced. "Padre Pio was not alone. I saw Jesus in Padre Pio, and Padre Pio in Jesus, who formed one thing. I looked at the appearance of the one and the other: Padre Pio more transparent and wonderful, and the face of Jesus with the Nazarene hair, which was a marvel, and I remained enchanted looking at them!"

Daniele now did not think he was worthy to kiss that heart. But Padre Pio, instead, took the Brother's head once more and placed it over the wound. "And I kiss and kiss, but I do it with more ardor, with more love, thinking that I kissed at the same time the side of Jesus and the side of Padre Pio." Then very slowly he pulled himself away. He no longer felt the anxiety he had felt before, but also the double presence had gone.

"Perhaps because my heart was by now full, and looking at the Padre, I saw only his person." Padre Pio looked at him and asked if he was content now. Daniele replied: "Padre, only Jesus whom I saw in you, could repay you for that great and wonderful grace which you have granted me this night."

Whenever extraordinary events happened, Daniele would tell them to Padre Agostino, to seek his advice on how to discern them and behave. Padre Agostino was the confessor and spiritual director of Padre Pio. On this occasion, he importuned Daniele: "I beg you son, ask Padre Pio for confirmation of what has happened to you, because sometimes the enemy (the devil) can put his tail on it." Therefore, Daniele decided to seek a definite confirmation from Padre Pio, in order to be certain that what had occurred that night was true and real.

He sought this confirmation on several occasions, but Padre Pio was evasive in answering. One evening, when the rest of the friars were at dinner, he was keeping the Padre company on the little terrace near his cell. Following a moment of silence, Daniele said to him, "Father, what happened the other night, was it true or was . . ." But before he could finish, Padre Pio interrupted him, while gazing out towards the countryside below the Gargano mountain, and he began to talk about the beauty of the evening. "Look at that moon as it is reflected in the Gulf of Manfredonia, it seems we are so close by. It is like a mirror in which we can reflect ourselves. These are the works of God!" And he proceeded to praise the wonders of the Lord. Daniele listened respectfully, but his mind was bent on having that confirmation. He thought to himself that as soon as Padre Pio stops talking, he will ask him again, but that evening nothing more could be done.

The very next night they were sitting on the terrace again, and Daniele said to him, "Father, I would like the confirmation of the other night . . ." But once more Padre Pio did not acknowledge the request, and instead began to describe the distant city of Foggia in the plains below, which that evening was well illuminated and could be clearly seen.

A few days later everyone was in choir to recite the Vespers prayers. But Daniele, instead of concentrating on praying, continued to think about the need for confirmation, to be sure that what had happened was not a trick of the devil. In his thoughts, he mentally asked Padre Pio if the events of that evening were true, and Padre Pio, ever so slightly, nodded his head in the affirmative. But Daniele still was not satisfied. He sought a clearer, more secure confirmation, and once again mentally repeated the same request. This time Padre Pio slowly turned towards him, and in the midst of the praying friars, said in a voice loud enough for everyone to hear, "Oh, now is this enough?" Daniele was full of joy and began laughing, finally satisfied with this confirmation, while the Father Superior rushed over to ask Padre Pio what had happened.

The cause for the canonization of the Servant of God, Brother Daniele Natale, has begun. His mortal remains have been transferred to a place near the altar of Padre Pio's church of Santa Maria delle Grazie in San Giovanni Rotondo.

This article is based on Brother Natale's own account of his experience, which can be found found at the Internet website of the *Friends of Fra Natale* *http://www.amicidifradaniele.it/sito/*.

NOVENA PRAYER OF PADRE PIO

(This novena prayer was recited every day by Padre Pio for all those who asked his prayers)

I. O my Jesus, You have said, 'Truly I say to you, ask and it will be given you, seek and you will find, knock and it will be opened to you.' Behold, I knock, I seek and ask for the grace of...

Our Father... Hail Mary... Glory be to the Father...
Sacred Heart of Jesus, I place all my trust in you.

II. O my Jesus, You have said, 'Truly I say to you, if you ask anything of the Father in my name, He will give it to you.' Behold, in Your name, I ask the Father for the grace of...

Our Father... Hail Mary... Glory be to the Father...

Sacred Heart of Jesus, I place all my trust in you.

III. O my Jesus, You have said, 'Truly I say to you, heaven and
earth will pass away but my words will not pass away.'
Encouraged by Your infallible words, I now ask for the grace of…

Our Father… Hail Mary… Glory be to the Father…
Sacred Heart of Jesus, I place all my trust in you.

O Sacred Heart of Jesus, for whom it is impossible not to have
compassion on the afflicted, have pity on us poor sinners
and grant us the grace which we ask of You, through the Sorrowful and Immaculate heart of Mary, Your tender mother and ours.

Hail, Holy Queen… St. Joseph, foster father of Jesus, pray for us

BIBLIOGRAPHY

Allegri, Renzo, *I Miracoli di Padre Pio*, Milan, Arnaldo Mondadori, 1993.

Allegri, Renzo, *Padre Pio Il Santo dei Miracoli*, Milan, Arnaldo Mondadori, 2002.

Allen, Diane, *Pray, Hope and Don't Worry*, San Diego, Aventine Press, 2009.

Carty, Rev. Charles Mortimer, *Padre Pio: The Stigmatist*, Rockford, IL., Tan Books and Publishers, Inc., 1973.

Chiocci, Francobaldo and Cirri, Luciano, *Padre Pio Storia D'una Vittima,* Roma, I libri del NO, 1967.

D'Apolito, Alberto, *Padre Pio of Pietrelcina: Memories, Experiences, Testimonials*, San Giovanni Rotondo, Editions: Padre Pio of Pietrelcina,1986.

Del Fante, Alberto, *Per La Storia*, Bologna, Anonima Arti Grafiche, 1948.

Festa, Giorgio, *Misteri di Scienza e Luci di Fede*, Roma, Star, 1949.

Fisher, Eric, *Healing Miracles*, London, Harper Collins, 1993.

Friends of Fra Natale, *http://www.amicidifradaniele.it/sito/*.

Gaeta, Irene, *http://www.idiscepolidipadrepio.it/index.php?lang=en*

Gallagher, Jim, *Padre Pio: The Pierced Priest*, London, Harper Collins, 1995.

Giacometti, Giulio and Sessa, Piera, *Padre Pio Mistero e Miracolo*, Pessano, Mimep-Docete 2015.

Malatesta, Enrico, *I Miracoli che hanno fatto Santo Padre Pio*, Casale Monferrato, Italy, Edizioni Piemme, 1998.

Malatesta, Enrico, *L'Ultimo Segreto di Padre Pio*, Casale Monferrato, Italy, Edizioni Piemme, 1997.

Malatesta, Enrico, *La Vera Storia di Padre Pio*, Casale Monferrato, Italy, Edizioni Piemme, 1999.

McCaffery, John, *The Friar of San Giovanni: Tales of Padre Pio*, London, Darton, Longman & Todd, Ltd., 1978.

Morcaldi, Cleonice, *La Mia Vita Vicino a Padre Pio*, Rome, Edizioni Dehoiane, 1997.

Padre Pio of Pietrelcina, *Letters Vol III*, San Giovanni Rotondo, Editions: Padre Pio of Pietrelcina,1994.

Parente, Fr. Alessio OFM Cap., *"Send Me Your Guardian Angel,"* Amsterdam N.Y., The Noteworthy Company, 1983.

Parente, Fr. Alessio OFM Cap., *The Holy Souls "Viva Padre Pio,"* San Giovanni Rotondo, Editions: Padre Pio of Pietrelcina, 1990.

Ruffin, Bernard, *Padre Pio: The True Story (Revised and Expanded)*, Huntington, IN, Our Sunday Visitor, 1991.

Schug, John A., *A Padre Pio Profile*, Petersham, MA, St. Bede's Publications, 1987.

Voce di Padre Pio magazine, San Giovanni Rotondo, February and March, 1995, January 1996, December 2007.

Winowska, Maria, *The True Face of Padre Pio*, London, The Catholic Book Club, 1961.

Zavala, Jose Maria, Padre Pio *I Miracoli Sconosciuti del Santo con le Stigmate,* Torino, La Fontana di Siloe, 2013.

ABOUT THE AUTHOR

Frank M. Rega is a Third Order Franciscan, a Knight of Columbus, and the author of many books and articles on Catholic saints and mystics, including St. Padre Pio, St. Francis of Assisi, St. Peter, and Luisa Piccarreta. A Phi Beta Kappa graduate of Rutgers University, he studied for a year at Yale's Institute for Human Relations on a Woodrow Wilson Fellowship. Before his retirement to Delaware, he was a software consultant for Compuware Corporation, working on projects for NASA and the Department of Homeland Security.

Frank's gateway web page is www.frankrega.com and his email address is regaf@aya.yale.edu.

Printed in Great Britain
by Amazon